MEDITATIONS ON THE SACRED HEART

COMMENTARY & MEDITATIONS on THE DEVOTION
OF THE FIRST FRIDAYS, THE APOSTLESHIP OF
PRAYER, THE HOLY HOUR

REV. JOSEPH McDONNELL, SJ

SENSUS FIDELIUM PRESS

Gastonia, North Carolina

ISBN: 978-1-962639-64-4

For more information, please visit sensusfideliumpress.com

Nihil Obstat.

H. SEBASTIANUS BOWDEN,
Censor Deputatus.

Imprimatur.

EDM. CAN. SURMONT,
Vicarius Generalis.
Westmonasterii,
Die 3 Februarii, **1913.**

FOREWORD

THE following pages may naturally be divided into four parts: two novenas of meditations on the Sacred Heart, with special reference to the devotion of the First Fridays; a novena of meditations on the kindred subject of the Apostleship of Prayer; and a brief account of the devotional exercise of the Holy Hour, with accompanying meditations. This latter exercise is very intimately associated with the Apostleship of Prayer.

These constituent portions of the book were not all written at the same time, nor was it my original intention to combine them into one. This was an afterthought, suggested by some persons who considered that the gathering together of these meditations in a single book would prove of use to many fervent clients of the Sacred Heart. I hope this explanation may suffice for those who discover any want of unity or continuity of treatment in the meditations.

Indeed, the division into three novenas is not without its own advantages. Furthermore, these twenty-seven meditations, together with the four devoted to the Holy Hour, making thirty-one in all, supply sufficient matter for an entire Month of Meditations on the Sacred Heart. The book may thus be used as a book of Meditations for the Month of June.

The "Points for Self-Examination" given in connection with the first nine meditations, as well as some of the matter of these meditations of the first series, are taken largely, at least in substance, from the very excellent Latin work Sacerdos, written many years ago by Father Petit, S.J., a well-known Belgian Jesuit.

May our Lord Himself vouchsafe to bless this effort, however small and unworthy, to promote devotion to His most Sacred Heart.

JOSEPH MCDONNELL, S.J.
FEAST OF THE PURIFICATION OF THE BLESSED VIRGIN,
February, 1913.

JESUS, MEEK AND HUMBLE OF HEART,
MAKE MY HEART LIKE UNTO THINE
(300 days ind. for each recital. — Pius X., Sept. 15, 1905)

TWELVE PROMISES MADE BY OUR LORD TO BLESSED MARGARET MARY IN FAVOUR OF THOSE DEVOTED TO HIS SACRED HEART

1. "I will give them all the graces necessary for their state of life."

2. "I will establish peace in their families."

3. "I will console them in all their difficulties."

4. "I will be their assured refuge in life, and more especially at death."

5. "I will pour out abundant benedictions on all their undertakings."

6. "Sinners shall find in My Heart an infinite ocean of mercy."

7. "Tepid souls shall become fervent."

8. "Fervent souls shall advance rapidly to great perfection."

9. "I will bless the houses in which the image of My Heart shall be exposed and honored."

10. "I will give to priests the power of touching the most hardened hearts."

11. "Persons who propagate this devotion, shall have their names inscribed in My Heart, and they shall never be effaced from It."

12. "I promise thee, in the excess of the mercy of My Heart, that Its all-powerful love will grant to all those who receive Communion on the First Friday of every Month, for nine consecutive months, the grace of final repentance, and that they shall not die under My displeasure, nor without receiving their Sacraments, and that My Heart shall be their secure refuge at that last hour."

CONTENTS

FIRST SERIES

THE DEVOTION OF THE FIRST FRIDAYS

INTRODUCTION.

The Devotion of the First Fridays—already so well-known and so widely diffused—has produced such wonderful results that it appears unnecessary to dwell on its advantages. As everyone knows, it has its origin in the Promise made by Christ to Blessed Margaret Mary in favor of all such as should worthily receive Communion on the First Friday of every month. It would be needless to recount the favors and graces of all kinds procured by the making of the First Friday Communions. Suffice it to say that wherever this devotion has been adopted it has produced, not merely in individuals but in entire parishes and communities, the most wonderful and consoling fruits of piety and holiness.

These Meditations on the Sacred Heart are each followed by a few short heads or points for practical self-examination on subjects connected with devotion to the Sacred Heart. Appropriate matter for spiritual reading, taken from the *Imitation,* is assigned at the end of each meditation. Finally, the prayers given at the conclusion of this first series of meditations are meant to be recited after Communion on each of the First Fridays.

N.B.—The Meditations, Examens, and Prayers given here may also, with great profit, be used as a Novena for the Feast of the Sacred Heart, or at other times of the year.

I.—THE REVELATION OF THE DEVOTION

1st Prelude.—Behold Christ appearing to Blessed Margaret Mary, and bidding her make known the devotion to the Sacred Heart.

2nd Prelude.—Ask for solid and persevering devotion to the Sacred Heart.

1st *Point.*—The Apparition.

2nd Point.—The words of Christ to Blessed Margaret Mary.

3rd Point.—Reasons for embracing the Devotion to the Sacred Heart.

1st Point.—The Apparition.

Consideration.—Three things deserve special notice in this apparition: (1) The *Person* who thus appeared. Christ did not send an angel to reveal to man the devotion to His Sacred Heart. He brought the tidings of this precious gift to us in Person. (2) The *end* and object of the apparition—namely, to set all hearts on fire with the love of God, and to communicate to us the priceless treasures of the Sacred Heart—treasures which, to use the words of Christ Himself, "contain graces of sanctification and salvation which suffice to free men from the abyss of perdition." (3) The *manner* of the apparition. Behold the rays, the flames, the cross, the thorns, the wound—all telling us in accents the most eloquent of the boundless love that fills the Heart of Jesus for each one of us.

Application.— "My Divine Heart," says Christ, "is so full of love for men that, unable any longer to contain within Itself these flames of burning love, It needs must spread them abroad, and make them known to men in order to enrich them with the treasures

It contains." Love tends to diffuse itself. If the love of Jesus really burns in my heart it will communicate itself to others. Am I an apostle of devotion to the Sacred Heart? Do I spread abroad the books and pictures, scapulars and badges, of the Sacred Heart? Am I a member of the *Apostleship of Prayer,* and do I make it known to others?

Affections and Resolutions.— "Who will grant me to travel over the whole earth to captivate all hearts to Thee. Let me become, I entreat Thee, the apostle of Thy Heart, that I may spread Thy Love everywhere" *(Imitation of the Sacred Heart).*

2nd Point.—The Words of Christ to Blessed Margaret Mary.

Consideration.—Listen to His *laments* as He complains of the ingratitude of men. "This ingratitude," He says to Blessed Margaret Mary, "wounds Me more than all else I endured during My Passion." Two things He asked of her in atonement for this ingratitude—namely, (1) That she would receive Holy Communion on the first Friday of each month; (2) that she would make the Holy Hour.

Listen, too, to His wonderful *promises* in favor of those who practice and propagate devotion to His Sacred Heart: "My Divine Master has shown me that the names of many were inscribed in letters of gold on His Sacred Heart, and that on this account He would never permit them to be effaced from It. The names are of those who, animated with the desire of procuring honor for His Sacred Heart, have earnestly labored to make It known and loved. ..." "The Heart of Jesus is pleased with your labors because He loves you!" *(Letters of Blessed Margaret Mary).*

Application.—Imagine that our Lord says to you as He said to Margaret Mary Alacoque: " Men show Me nothing but coldness and indifference, but do thou at least give Me pleasure by making atonement for their ingratitude. Go to Communion as an act of thanksgiving and reparation to My Sacred Heart every First Friday and make the Holy Hour in My honor."

Affections and Resolutions.—My dearest Jesus, let it be my happy privilege to bear Thee company in Thy abandonment and by my loving assiduity to assuage the sorrows of Thy Sacred Heart.

3rd Point.—Reasons for Embracing the Devotion to the Sacred Heart.

Consideration—First Reason.—It is the manifest will of Christ, made known (1) by His own sacred lips to Blessed Margaret Mary Alacoque; (2) by the authority of the Church, which has given its warmest approval to the practice of this devotion; (3) by the action of Divine Providence, which has wonderfully blessed this devotion. *Second Reason.*—It is an excellent means of advancing in perfection. Christ has promised, in favor of those who practice devotion to His Sacred Heart, that "the tepid will become fervent, whilst the fervent will attain to the highest perfection." Experience provides us with many instances of this. *Third Reason.*—It secures for us a true Friend—One to whom we can at all times have recourse, and who is most willing and powerful to help us. All other friends may abandon us, but the loving Heart of Jesus will never leave us. With a friend so devoted and so powerful, what have we to fear? *Fourth Reason.*—It is a pledge of our salvation. "Our Lord has made known to me," wrote Blessed Margaret Mary, "that no one who is devout to the Sacred Heart will be lost."

Application.—With so many and such powerful motives for embracing this devotion, will you any longer hesitate? "I say with certainty," again writes Blessed Margaret Mary, "that were it known how pleasing this devotion is to Jesus Christ, there is no one, however cold his love may be, who would not at once practice it."

Affections and Resolutions.—Sweet Heart of Jesus, do Thou make Thyself Master of all hearts. Reign over our hearts in spite of Thine enemies—in spite of our sinfulness, tepidity, and coldness.

Colloquy.

Spiritual Reading: *Imitation,* Book III., chapter, v.

POINTS FOR SELF-EXAMINATION.

1. On Purity of Heart.

2. Do I set before me in each confession some special fault to overcome until my next confession?

3. Do I make my daily examination of conscience faithfully and fruitfully, trying to *discover* my faults, to *be sorry* for them, to *amend* them? Do I choose out one special fault to which I am most subject, and examine myself on it in particular?

4. Do I guard my senses? They are the windows of the soul through which death enters.

5. Am I careful about my reading? my conversation? the companions I select? the places I frequent? Are any of these things occasions of sin to me?

6. Do I avoid idleness, which is the mother of many faults?

7. Dol use the two great helps to purity of heart: devotion and temperance?

8. Do I reject dangerous thoughts promptly, prayerfully, perseveringly? They are so many sparks from hell fire, which must be shaken off as we would shake off a burning spark from the grate.

9. Do I, in short, strive to keep my soul at all times a fitting receptacle for the Blessed Eucharist, by nourishing it with holy thoughts, prayer, and pious reading?

II.—THE CROWN OF THORNS THAT SURROUNDS THE SACRED HEART

1st Prelude.—Behold the Heart of Jesus surrounded with a Crown of Thorns.

2nd Prelude.—Ask grace to understand the meaning of this Crown of Thorns, and to learn the lessons it teaches.

St. Bernard distinguishes a fourfold crown that encircles the brow of Christ; we may consider the same fourfold crown as encircling His Sacred Heart.

1st *Point.*—The Crown of Sorrow.

2nd Point.—The Crown of Mercy.

3rd Point.—The Crown of Justice.

4th Point.—The Crown of Glory.

1st Point.—The Crown of Sorrow.

Consideration.—The Crown of cruel Thorns that pierced the Sacred Head of the Redeemer, and caused Him such unspeakable bodily anguish had its counterpart in the still more cruel Crown of Sorrow that pierced and lacerated His most tender and loving Heart. Its thorns were the sins and infidelities of those who were supposed to be devoted to Him, the treachery, indifference, or coldness of His chosen friends. "I looked," He says, "for one that would grieve together with Me, and there was none; and for one that would comfort Me, and I found none." (Psalm Ixviii., 21). "If My enemy had reviled me, I would verily have borne with it . . . but thou a man of one mind .... who didst take sweet meats together with Me." (Psalm liv., 13-15).

Application.—Christ once appeared to Blessed Margaret Mary all bleeding and covered with wounds, and He told her that He had received these wounds from souls that were specially devoted to His service. Have I been of the number? If so, what shall be my conduct for the future?

Affections and Resolutions.—My Jesus, if I have wounded Thy Sacred Heart by my sins, enable me to make reparation by my love.

2nd Point.—The Crown of Mercy.

Consideration.—The Crown of Mercy on the brow of the Redeemer was His tender solicitude for our salvation. The Crown of Mercy that surrounds His Sacred Heart is His deep sympathy and compassion for us in our sorrows. Here on earth the Heart of Jesus was full of tenderest compassion for every phase of misery and suffering. That loving Heart is still as tender and compassionate as ever.

Application.—Listen to the loving invitation of the Savior: "Come to Me, all you that labor, and are heavily burdened, and I will refresh you." In all your sorrows, trials, and afflictions seek your consolation in the Heart of Jesus. It is ever waiting to console you in the Tabernacle; to be your comfort and support in Holy Communion; to be the source of untold graces and blessings and an infinite sacrifice of expiation for your sins in the Holy Sacrifice of the Altar.

Affections and Resolutions.—"Lord, what have I besides Thee, and what do I desire outside of Thee?"

3rd Point.—The Crown of Justice.

Consideration.—The Crown of Justice on the Head of Christ is the full and glorious reparation that will be made to Him on the day of general judgment. The Crown of Justice on His Sacred Heart is the serene and invincible patience with which He endured the reproaches and outrages offered to Him in His Passion.

Application.—Let the thought of all that I have done to wound the Sacred Heart of Jesus in the past inspire me with patience to endure the little trials of my earthly pilgrimage. If Christ suffered so much in atonement for my sins, shall I be unwilling to endure anything to make atonement for them?

Affections and Resolutions.—Think of your sins, and of all that Christ suffered for them, when you are inclined to murmur.

4th Point.—The Crown of Glory.

The Crown of Glory on the brow of Christ is the diadem of everlasting glory which He gained on earth by His labors, sufferings, and humiliations. The Crown of Glory that encircles His Sacred Heart is the never-ending and unbounded bliss that thrills through its every fiber at the thought of all He did and suffered for our sakes on earth.

Application.—This same bright Crown of Glory awaits each one of us in heaven. A few short years of loving, patient labor here on earth, and then a crown of everlasting bliss in heaven! All depends on how I spend the fleeting moments of my earthly trial. Think how short is the longest life when compared to eternity, and you will agree with St. Paul that the "sufferings of this time are not worthy to be compared with the glory to come that shall be revealed in us." (Romans viii. 18)

Affections and Resolutions.—"Lord, I desire to be dissolved and to be with Thee." Keep your heart and mind ever fixed on your eternal home.

Colloquy.

Spiritual Reading: *Imitation,* Book III., chapters, xlviii., xlix.

POINTS FOR SELF-EXAMINATION.

On Devotion to the Passion.

"If we suffer with Christ, we shall also reign with Him," says St. Paul. We can suffer practically with Christ in two ways:

1. *By devotion to the memorials of the Passion.*

These are:

(a) The Crucifix: Do I keep it before me when writing, reading, working, and especially praying? Do I often press it with devotion to my lips, and reverence it?

(b) The Sign of the Cross: Do I make it devoutly and attentively, or in a hurried, careless way? Do I use it as a protection against my spiritual enemies? Do I make it frequently?

(c) The pictures, medals, badges, statues, etc., of the Sacred Heart: Remembering the promise of Our Lord to those who show honor to these images; great graces are sometimes got by wearing a badge or scapular of the Sacred Heart. Do I reverence, and pray before, the pictures and statues of the Sacred Heart? Give them to children and others? Recommend their erection in houses?

(d) The Via Crucis or Stations of the Cross: To perform this devotion often, keeps one fervent, is very pleasing to the Sacred Heart, and procures great relief for souls in purgatory.

2. The second way of suffering with Christ is to *unite our sufferings with His,* and to try to bear them as He bore them.

We suffer either in our *soul,* or in our *body,* or in our *honor.*

In my *soul:* How do I bear sorrow, anxiety, depression, loneliness, worry, and other mental trials? In my *body:* Am I restless and impatient under physical suffering, disease, fatigue, sleeplessness, heat, and cold? In my *honor:* How do I behave under false accusations, or suspicions, calumny, loss of reputation, coldness, or forgetfulness of friends, etc?

Jesus, grant me grace to suffer with Thee here that I may reign with Thee hereafter.

III.—THE LANCE AND THE WOUNDED HEART OF JESUS

1st Prelude.—Behold the scene depicted by St. John in his Gospel: "But after they were come to Jesus, when they saw that He was already dead, they did not break His legs. But one of the soldiers with a spear opened His side, and immediately there came out blood and water."—(John xix. 33, 34).

2nd Prelude.—Grant me grace, 0 Lord, to enter into the Wound of Thy Sacred Heart, and there to make my dwelling forever.

1st *Point.*—The lance is the instrument of Divine Providence.

2nd *Point.*—The instrument of Love.

3rd *Point.*—The instrument of Power.

1st Point.—The Lance the Instrument of Divine Providence.

Consideration.—Our merciful Redeemer, worn out by hours of bitter agony, had at length breathed forth His Soul into the Hands of His Eternal Father. His Blessed Body hung lifeless on the cross, when a soldier, we are told, approached and drove his lance into the Heart of our Divine Lord, "and immediately," says the Gospel, "there came out blood and water." (John xix. 34).

Application.—What was the intention of the Roman soldier in this cruel action? None other than to satisfy his malice. What was our loving Savior's intention? It was to open to us for evermore a never-failing source and fountain of all graces, and to show that He had shed the last drop of His most Precious Blood, and that love and generosity could go no further. In this mysterious opening of His Sacred Side, Christ teaches me three important lessons: (1) To be generous with Him as He has been so generous with me. (2) To seek in the wounded Heart of Jesus strength and courage in my weakness, comfort in my sorrows, light in my perplexities, sorrow and forgiveness for my manifold offences. (3) To learn to have unbounded confidence and trust in Divine Providence, which knows so well how to draw good out of evil, sweets from bitters, joy from sorrows, triumph from humiliation. Thoughts like these will strengthen and support me in hours of darkness and affliction.

Affections and Resolutions.—"O Lord, it is good for us to have sometimes troubles and adversities, for they make us enter into our own hearts; they remind us that we are in exile; they teach us not to place our hopes and joys in the empty, fleeting things of earth" (a Kempis).

2nd Point.—The Lance the Instrument of Love.

Consideration.—"I have come to cast fire on the earth, and what will I but that it be kindled"; thus it is Jesus speaks to me from off the Cross in accents sweet and eloquent. From out His Wounded Heart came forth the fire of love that was to kindle with its flames the heart of the Apostle and the Confessor, the Virgin and the Martyr.

Application.—Fix your eyes upon the Heart of Jesus, and behold the fiery ardors bursting through the open Wound with the irresistible impetuosity of a love that knows no bounds. It is a very furnace of consuming love, that seeks to get possession of my poor cold heart, and purge it of its rust and dross, and set it all aglow with love. That fiery furnace burns upon my tongue and glows within my bosom every time I have the happiness of receiving the Blessed Body of my Savior in the Eucharist. Is it possible that I can so often approach this furnace of the love of Christ and not be set on fire with its flames!

Affections and Resolutions.—"If I cannot as yet be all on fire like the Cherubim and Seraphim, I will yet endeavor to apply myself to devotion and to prepare my heart, that in the humble reception of this life-giving Sacrament, I may seek some flame, however small, from this divine fire" (a Kempis).

3rd Point.—The Lance the Instrument of Power.

Consideration.—We, too, as did the Roman soldier of old, hold in our hands a lance with which we can open for ourselves the life-giving fountains of the Sacred Heart. The lance we hold is not of steel or iron; it is a spiritual lance of double edge, whose point is keen to open for us the hidden treasures of the Heart of Jesus. It is the spiritual lance of *confidence* and deep *humility:* unbounded confidence and trust in the never-failing love and merits of our Savior; profound humility and absolute distrust of self.

By confidence and trust in God we do a sort of violence to the divine and loving Heart of Christ, and force Him, in a manner, to pour down upon our souls the treasures of His love, for "Know ye that no one hath hoped in the Lord and hath been confounded" (Ecclesiasticus ii., 11). By humility we attract towards ourselves the merciful glance of Him "Who hath exalted the humble, and hath filled the hungry with good things" (Luke i. 52, 53).

Application.—Confidence in God's unbounded love, humility and absolute distrust of self, these are the virtues that will enable me to penetrate into the wounded Heart of Jesus, and there to find the strength and grace that will enable me to do great things in His service.

Affections and Resolutions.—"In Thee, O Lord, I place all my hope, to Thee I look for help in all my tribulations and anguish, for I find all to be infirm and unstable whatever I behold outside of Thee" (a Kempis).

Colloquy.

Spiritual Reading: *Imitation,* Book II., chapter. viii.

POINTS FOR SELF-EXAMINATION.

On Fervor of Spirit.

1. Are the *characteristic marks* of fervor found in me?

(1) Pure intention; (2) whole-hearted *devotion to my work;* (3) attention to the *presence of God;* (4) vigorous *effort* in difficulties; (5) *perseverance;* (6) desire to *sanctify* myself; (7) effort to *avoid lesser faults*; (8) *anxiety* in all things to *know* and *do God's will;* (9) *readiness to do* and *suffer* much *for God.*

2. Are the *effects* of fervor found in me?

(1) Love of *labor*; (2) *patience* in sufferings and trials; (3) *delicacy of conscience;* (4) practical desire and *effort to advance God's glory* and the *interests of the Sacred Heart;* (5) *charity* in thought, word, and action; (6) *generosity* towards God; (7) *spirit of prayer* and *self-denial.*

3. Do I use the *means* necessary to keep alive fervor of spirit?

(10 Devotion to the Sacred Heart and fidelity to its practices; (2) faithful and fervent performance of my *daily duties;* (3) devotion to *prayer,* the *Sacraments,* spiritual *reading,* practices of *self-denial;* aiming at a *high standard.*

IV.—THE EMOTIONS OF THE SACRED HEART

1st Prelude.—Imagine Jesus saying to you, as He said to Blessed Margaret Mary: " Behold this Heart, which has loved men so much."

2nd Prelude.—Ask for grace to understand and sympathize with the emotions of the Sacred Heart.

There are three classes of emotions in the Sacred Heart:—

1st Point.—Sorrows of the Sacred Heart.

2nd Point.—Its Joys.

3rd Point—Its Desires.

1ST POINT.—THE SORROWS OF THE SACRED HEART.

Consideration.—Jesus Christ finds, in a greater or less degree, in my soul, six things which cause sorrow to His Sacred Heart: (1) My tepidity and want of earnestness and energy in His service. (2) My indifference to His loving invitations. (3) My inconstancy and unfaithfulness to my good resolutions. (4) My pusillanimity, which prevents me from embarking on any great enterprise in His service, makes me diffident and distrustful in spite of all His promises, and causes me to give up at the slightest breath of opposition or adversity. (5) My sins, which tend to raise a barrier between me and His Sacred Heart. (6)

My want of zeal in promoting His interests in the hearts of others, especially of children and those entrusted to my care.

Application.—Examine yourself on each of these six things, and see how far they exist in you, and how far in consequence you have had a share in adding to the sorrows of the Sacred Heart.

Affections and Resolutions.—Dearest Jesus, if hitherto I have done little else than grieve Thy Sacred Heart, I will now, at length, consecrate myself entirely to Thee, and, wholly relying on Thy all-powerful assistance, I will strive to become both a true disciple and a zealous apostle of devotion to Thy Sacred Heart.

2ND POINT.—THE JOYS OF THE SACRED HEART.

Consideration.—There are, in like manner, six things which Jesus finds in the hearts of His true and faithful friends, which bring joy and consolation to His Sacred Heart: (1) Fervor and earnestness in His service. This is the practical expression of my love, which, as St. Ignatius says, consists rather in works, in willingness to labor and make sacrifices, than in words. (2) Conformity of will, especially in times of sorrow and adversity, and a loving solicitude in all things to second His desires. (3) Fidelity to my good resolutions, even when it costs me something to be faithful to them. (4) Unbounded and unswerving trust and confidence in the boundless love and goodness of the Sacred Heart. Animated with this disposition, I shall undertake, and successfully accomplish, great things for the honor of the Heart of Jesus. I shall never stop at anything that I know to be His will. (5) Patience in adversity, humble submission to the will of God in sorrow, disappointment, or bereavement. (6) Ardent, practical, and prudent zeal, which never tires of working for the Master, and is ever striving, "in season and out of season," to promote His interests.

Application. — How far is this a picture of my dispositions? When Jesus lay in mortal agony, beneath the pale green olives of Gethsemani, it is believed that the consoling angel placed before Him visions of the holy souls that would hereafter strive to make amends for all the wickedness and indifference of men. Was I among the number? Do I wish to be so?

Affections and Resolutions.—O Lord, to Thee I offer up and consecrate my heart. Banish from it all that is offensive to Thee; fill it with the disposition that will make it pleasing to Thy Sacred Heart.

3RD POINT.—THE DESIRES OF THE HEART OF JESUS.

Consideration.—Among the many desires that fill the breast of Jesus, there are three in particular that regard me in my relations to His Sacred Heart: (1) Christ ardently longs for my sanctification, that thus my devotion to His Sacred Heart may be more acceptable and pleasing to His sight, and that I may become a fitter instrument to propagate this devotion in the hearts of others. (2) He desires that I cultivate within my soul a very true and solid devotion to His Sacred Heart, seeing that unless I myself am animated in a high degree with this devotion I cannot hope to kindle it in others. (3) Hence, He wishes me to be not merely ardently devoted to His Sacred Heart myself, but to be, moreover, its apostle in the hearts of all with whom I come in contact.

Application.—I have sins to atone for, graces and favors innumerable to be thankful for, a threefold battle—against the world, the flesh, and the devil—to fight here, and an eternal inheritance to secure hereafter. All these ends may be powerfully promoted by devotion to the Sacred Heart: it expiates sin, for its exercises are all exercises of Divine love, which, as theologians teach, possesses the power of expiation; it is a means of thanksgiving, for this, with reparation, are the two chief ends of the devotion; it helps me to fight the battle here and to win the crown hereafter, since its effect is to elevate the soul from a state of tepidity to one of fervor, and to infuse spiritual energy and vigor into languid souls.

Affections and Resolutions.—Teach me, O Lord, to understand the sorrows, joys, and desires of Thy Sacred Heart, that I may strive to lessen the one and to increase the others.

Colloquy.

Spiritual Reading: Imitation, Book I., chapter xxv.

POINTS FOR SELF-EXAMINATION.
THE SIGNS OF ADVANCEMENT IN SPIRIT.

In spiritual things not to advance is to go back. In order to see if you are advancing, consider the following Eight Signs of Spiritual Progress:

1st Sign.—Diminution of sin: are your sins fewer and less serious?

2nd Sign.—Victory over temptations: do you resist promptly, prayerfully, perseveringly?

3rd Sign.—Curbing of evil passions: are you gaining greater mastery over them?

4th Sign.—Rooting out bad habits : have you less inclination towards them? Greater facility in overcoming them? Greater desire for purity of soul?

5th Sign.—Ordinary actions done with greater perfection: less from mere habit, with greater purity of intention, with fewer faults, with more diligence.

6th Sign.—Increase of good habits: are your good actions performed more promptly and easily, with less repugnance of self-love, with more pleasure, with greater constancy.

7th Sign.—Less affection for the things of earth : are your joys and consolations more spiritual and less of this world, are you less dependent on the pleasures of the senses?

8th Sign.—Greater love of recollection and silence: are you fonder of prayer, of visiting the Blessed Sacrament, of spiritual reading, of practices of devo-tion and self-denial?

O Jesus, grant that by means of devotion to Thy Sacred Heart I may rapidly advance in Thy service.

V.—ON ABANDONING ONESELF TO THE SACRED HEART

1st Prelude.—Behold St. Francis Xavier as he lies dying by the seashore on the Island of Sancian, abandoned by all, exclaiming in the boundless love of his heart: "In Thee, O Lord, have I hoped; let **me never** be confounded." (Psalm xxx., 2).

2nd Prelude.—Grace to abandon yourself wholly and unreservedly to the Sacred Heart.

1st *Point.*—The excellence of this self-abandonment.

2nd Point.—Its practice.

1st Point.—Excellence of this Self-abandonment.

Consideration.—How *happy* is the soul that thus resigns itself entirely into God's hands. No evil can befall it, for it is under the immediate guidance of God's Omnipotence. Nothing can oppose its will, for it has no other will or wish than that of God Himself. No enemies can hurt it, for God's almighty arm is its strong defense. How *securely* does it ride amidst the tempest and the storm. The winds may roar and the lightnings flash and the angry waves may threaten to engulf it, but even as of old the disciples rode securely in their bark across the waters of the lake, because they had with them the Lord and Master of the winds and waves, so the soul that places all its trust in God ever rests securely in the powerful and loving arms of Providence. How *dear* to God is such a soul. He watches when it sleeps, toils when it rests, anticipates its wants listens to its prayers, shares in its griefs comforts it in sorrow, guides it in doubt, guards it in danger, helps it in its enterprises, brings them to a happy issue, and carries it triumphantly over obstacles and dangers till it comes into the haven of eternal rest.

Application.—Nourish in your heart the spirit of abandonment of self into the hands of God. It is one of the most perfect forms of conformity to God's will, one of the highest exercises of devotion to the Sacred Heart. It is a source of profound peace, a pledge of salvation, a powerful and lasting bond of union with the Sacred Heart.

Affections and Resolutions.—"My God and my All!" "In Thee, O Lord, have I hoped; let me never be confounded." "To Thee, O Lord, I commit the wants of this perishable body; to Thee I entrust the more precious interests of my immortal soul. Though my faults are many, my misery great, my spiritual poverty extreme, my hope in Thee surpasses all; it is superior to my weakness, greater than any difficulties, stronger than death" (Father de la Colombiere).

2nd Point.—The Practice of Self-abandonment into God's Hands.

Consideration.—I am troubled with doubts and anxieties: shall I be lost or saved? Am I in God's friendship or not? Am I advancing or going back? My mind is all in darkness, I know not what to think, or what to say, or how to act. All I can do is to cry to Thee, O Sacred Heart, from the depths of my soul. O *Lord, I love Thee alone, I desire Thee alone, I abandon myself entirely to Thee.*

My enemies surround me, my friends abandon me, calumniators have robbed me of my character, my soul is flooded with a sea of sorrow and affliction, my heart is bowed down with woe, I have no one to comfort me, no one to advise me, I seem to stand alone and without a friend in the world. Yet from the depths of my sorrow and bereavement to Thee do I cry aloud, and say: O *Sacred Heart of Jesus, I love Thee alone, I desire Thee alone, I abandon myself entirely to Thee.*

I may have health or sickness, a happy life or one of sorrow, prosperity or failure, affluence or poverty, long life or short life, peace or contention of spirit; all this I heed not, my sole desire is to do Thy will. O *Sacred Heart of Jesus, I love Thee alone, I desire Thee alone, I abandon myself entirely to Thee.*

Application.—In all the events of life, its joys and sorrows, hopes and fears, the loving hand of Providence is ever guiding and protecting those who place their entire trust in God. The waves of tribulation threaten every moment to engulf you; but fear not, Christ is with you, even though He seems to sleep.

Affections and Resolutions.—"Though temptations should assail me, I will hope in Thee; though I should sink beneath my weakness, I will hope in Thee still; though I should break my resolutions, I will look to Thee confidently for grace to keep them in the end; though Thou shouldst kill me, even then will I trust in Thee; for Thou art my Father, my God, the support of my salvation; Thou art my kind, my tender and indulgent Parent, and I am Thy loving child who cast myself into Thy arms, and beg Thy blessing; who put my trust in Thee, and so trusting shall not be confounded" (Father de la Colombiere).

Colloquy.

Spiritual Reading: *Imitation,* Book III., chapter xxxvii.

POINTS FOR SELF-EXAMINATION.

On Preparing for Death.

"Blessed are the dead who die in the Lord." This can be said of those who, in greater or less degree as their state demands, are dead to the *world,* to the *flesh,* to *themselves.*

1. Am I dead to the *world?*—the world is the inordinate love of *riches, honors,* and *pleasures.* (1) Am I dead to the inordinate love of *riches?* of material comforts? Am I too expensive in my habits? Do I give enough alms? Do I spend too much on myself, too little on the poor? (2) *Honors.* Am I too ambitious and self-seeking? too solicitous about the good opinion of others? too downcast under humiliations? too much influenced by human respect? (3) *Pleasures.* Do I devote too much time to amusement? Do I seek it with too great avidity, and to the detriment of my duties?

2. Am I dead to the *flesh?*—that is to say, to the sinful or disorderly indulgence of the senses—eyes, ears, tongue, touch, taste? How do I use each of these senses? is any one of them a source of offence to God?

3. Am I dead to *myself?* Am I unduly devoted to my own will and judgment? proud? selfish? apt to criticize or despise others?

VI.—THE IMAGE OF THE SACRED HEART

1st Prelude.—Behold the Sacred Heart as it was shown by Christ Himself to Blessed Margaret Mary, full to overflowing with vigorous life, wounded in the side, crowned with thorns, surmounted with a cross, with flames issuing from it, surrounded with rays of light.

2nd Prelude.—**O** loving Heart of my Savior, enable me to draw most precious fruit from the contemplation of these symbols that surround Thee.

1st *Point.*—The Sacred Heart a living heart.

2nd Point.—The rays, the flames, the thorns.

3rd *Point.*—The cross, the gaping wound.

1st Point.—The Sacred Heart a Living Heart.

Consideration.—The Heart of Jesus is not a dead or lifeless heart, it is a real, living Heart of Flesh, hypostatically united with the Divine Word. Such is the Heart that Christ has given to me in His ardent love. He asks for mine in return: "Child, give Me thy heart." But He wants from me a heart that is living and vigorous, not dead in sin, nor sickly and languid with tepidity and venial faults.

Application.—If you wish to make an offering of your heart to Christ in such a manner as to please Him, you must free it, first, from fully deliberate sin; secondly, as far as may be from inordinate attachment to the things of earth. The love that animates it must be practical; that is, expressed in deeds, in willingness to labor and to suffer, rather than in mere words or barren professions of devotion. Has it been so hitherto? How about the future?

Affections and Resolutions.—Lord, for love of Thee I am ready to do and suffer all things, to receive from Thy hands what is hard and bitter, and in all things to be resigned to Thy most holy Will.

2nd Point.—The Rays, the Flames, the Thorns.

Consideration.—Devotion to the Sacred Heart has three remarkable effects upon the soul: it *illumines, inflames, assimilates.* It illumines the intellect to better understand and realize in deeper faith the fundamental truths of our religion; it inflames the will to act more efficaciously and energetically in accordance with the deep conviction of the intellect; it urges us to imitation of our crucified Redeemer, and thus assimilates our lives to His. These three effects we may consider to be typified by the rays, the flames, the thorns, that surround the Sacred Heart.

Application.—Is your devotion to the Sacred Heart of Jesus genuine and solid, or is it a mere affectionate emotion of the heart? Ask yourself this question seriously and answer it honestly. Your devotion is genuine if it produces the three effects already mentioned, especially if it shows itself practically in deeds, in willingness to labor and to suffer, in greater resignation to God's will in time of sorrow; in a word, if it tends to make you somewhat less unlike your crucified Redeemer.

Affections and Resolutions.—"Teach me, O Sacred Heart, to know Thee, that knowing Thee I may love Thee, that loving Thee I may imitate Thee" *(Spiritual Exercises* of St. Ignatius).

3rd Point.—The Cross, the Open Wound.

Consideration.—Why is the Sacred Heart represented to us as surmounted by a cross? To remind us that the cross must be the badge and mark of all true lovers of the Sacred Heart. It has ever been the distinctive characteristic of the saints and friends of Christ. Our Blessed Lady and St. Joseph bore a heavier cross through life than ever fell to human lot to carry. In the open wound of the Sacred Heart, we have an everlasting pledge of God's unbounded love for us, a refuge in sorrow, a means of atoning for sin, a fountain of graces.

Application.—"In the cross is salvation; in the cross is life; in the cross is protection from thine enemies; in the cross is infusion of heavenly sweetness; in the cross is strength of mind; in the cross is joy of spirit. . . . There is no health of soul or hope of eternal life but in the cross" (a Kempis). What reasons I have for rejoicing if God has laid the cross on me!

Affections and Resolutions.—O Sacred Heart of my Savior, I accept as from Thee whatsoever trials and crosses Thou art pleased to send. "In Thy Sacred Wound hide me, and never permit me to be separated from Thee" (Prayer of St. Ignatius).

Colloquy.

Spiritual Reading: *Imitation,* Book II., chapters xi., xii.

POINTS FOR SELF-EXAMINATION.

On Devotion to the Sacred Heart.

1. Do I clearly understand the end and object of the devotion?—*i.e.,* to *return thanks* to Christ for all He has done for me and others, and to *make reparation* for the injuries that I and others have inflicted on His Sacred Heart.

2. Is my devotion *practical?*—(1) *Each Day:* Do I make the "offering" of the *Apostleship Leaflet?* Say the decade for the Pope's intention? Renew my morning offering during the day? Make occasional visits of Reparation? Aspirations? (2) *Each Week:* Do I consecrate Friday to the Sacred Heart, doing something special on that day? (3) *Each Month:* How do I practice the First Friday Communion? Reparation Communion of the Third Degree? Acts of Consecration and Reparation? Benediction? (4) *Each Year:* How do I observe the Feast? Novena before it?

3. Am I an *apostle* of the devotion? Do I induce others to make the First Friday Communion? To join the *Apostleship of Prayer?* To read the *Messenger?* Practice the *Three Degrees* on the *Apostleship Leaflet?* In a word, am I striving to earn the rich reward promised by Jesus Christ to the *apostles* of His Sacred Heart? *"Those who propagate this devotion shall have their names written in My Heart, and they shall never be effaced."*

VII.—ON THE LOVE OF THE SACRED HEART OF JESUS FOR EACH OF US

1st Prelude.—To fix my thoughts I will imagine myself kneeling beside the Blessed Margaret Mary Alacoque in the little convent chapel of Paray-le-Monial at the moment when our Divine Lord appeared to her, and, showing her His Sacred Heart all burning with flames of the most ardent love, said to her these beautiful and touching words: "Behold this Heart, which has loved men so much."

2nd Prelude.—Say, with all possible fervor and devotion: "O Sacred Heart of Jesus, I implore, that I may ever love Thee more and more."

Let us consider the three following points:—

1st *Point.*—Who is this that loves me so much?

2nd *Point.*—Who and what am I that I should be the object of His love?

3rd *Point.*—In what manner has He loved Me?

1st Point.—Who is This that Loves Me so Much?

Consideration.—It is Jesus Christ, the Second Person of the Ever-Blessed Trinity, the God-made Man. It is the great Creator of the universe, the Lord and Sovereign Master of creation. It is a Being who is infinitely *wise*, infinitely *good*, infinitely *powerful*, infinitely *happy*; a Being who can in no way stand in need of me, to whose happiness, or power, or greatness, or glory, I cannot, except in a way that is entirely accidental and extrinsic to His nature, add in the slightest degree.

Application.—Hence the love of the Sacred Heart for me is purely *gratuitous* and wholly undeserved on my part. Am I ready, in return, to love our Divine Lord *gratis;* that is to say, when my love for Him demands some sacrifice, when I am left in dryness and desolation of spirit, without any feeling of sensible devotion? Am I ready, for His sake, to sacrifice my health, my reputation, my convenience, my life itself, if necessary? "A valiant lover of Christ," says a Kempis, "stands his ground in temptations ... As God pleases him in prosperity, so He displeases him not in adversity. A generous lover rests not in the gift, but in God over every gift."

Affections and Resolutions.—"O Sacred Heart of Jesus, teach me to be generous with Thee. Teach me to serve Thee as Thou deserves, to give and not to count the cost, to fight and not to heed the wounds, to toil and not to ask for rest, to labor and to seek no reward, save to feel that I do Thy will, O my God" (St. Ignatius).

2nd Point. — Who and what am I that I should be the object of His love?

I am an utterly *insignificant being*. What am I in comparison to the fourteen hundred millions of human beings that inhabit this earth? What is the population of the world when compared to the countless hosts of angels and saints in Paradise? What are all created beings in heaven, on earth, and in hell, when compared with God? What, therefore, am I in comparison with God? (St. Ignatius, *Spiritual Exercises*). Yet, that same God, in whose sight I am less than a grain of sand upon the seashore, lived, suffered, and died for me here on earth. He has become a daily Victim for my salvation in the Mass, a willing Prisoner in the Tabernacle, my heavenly Food and Sustenance in the Blessed Eucharist.

I am a *great sinner*. My soul is a foul and loathsome ulcer, from which is ever welling forth every species of poison and corruption. My sins are as a hideous leprosy that eats into the very vitals of my being and disfigures or destroys the noble image of the Godhead in my soul.

Application.—And yet, in spite of all my misery and wickedness, in spite of all my infidelity to grace, in spite of all my broken promises and pledges, and all the many times the Sacred Heart has raised me up and pardoned me, and I have again abandoned Him and fallen into sin, our Lord has never grown weary of me; He has never ceased to knock and wait in ever-anxious expectation at my door, and to whisper gentle words of loving earnest invitation to my soul, and say: *"Child, give Me thy heart."*

Affections and Resolutions.—"Lord, that I may know Thee, that I may know myself" (St. Augustine). Teach me, O Sacred Heart of Jesus, to realize Thy love, and to realize my own supreme unworthiness, ingratitude, and sinfulness. O Heart so full of love for me, fill my poor heart with love for Thee. Grant that I may show my love for Thee by never more offending Thee.

3rd Point.—In what Manner has the Sacred Heart Loved Me?

Consideration.—The Sacred Heart has loved me with a *genuine* love. It ardently longs for my salvation and sanctification, and has provided me abundantly with the means of securing my eternal happiness.

It loves me with a *generous* love, a love that knows no bounds save those which my own want of faith and confidence impose upon It. I have only to reflect a little on the innumerable graces and favors I have received from the Sacred Heart during my own past life to be convinced of this.

It loves me with a *constant,* never-failing love. In spite of all my sinfulness, and misery, and infidelity; in spite of diffidence, tepidity, and sloth; in spite of my broken promises and oft-repeated acts of infidelity; the Sacred Heart has never ceased to love me and to draw me by His gentle inspirations to His service.

Application.—I am very weak, very inconstant; I cannot trust myself. I am even as a child that weakly stumbles on by stony ways beset by many obstacles to bar its progress, and therefore have I need of some strong hand to hold me up and guide me, as I try to pick my slow and faltering steps along the rugged, thorny path that leads to heaven.

Affections and Resolutions.—Ah, yes, dear Lord, be Thou my guide. I place my hand in Thine that Thou mayest lead me as Thou wilt. I cannot see the hidden dangers that surround me. I know not of the cunning snares that lie along my path. Guide Thou my erring, aimless footsteps, till Thou brings me in safety to the Mount of God.

Colloquy.

Spiritual Reading: *Imitation,* Book II., chapter vii.

POINTS FOR SELF-EXAMINATION.

On the Practical Knowledge and Love of Jesus Christ.

How do I stand regarding the Person *of Jesus Christ?*

    1. In my *thoughts.*—Do I often think of our Lord? Do I meditate on the mysteries of His Life and Passion? Am I familiar with aspirations embodying the Sacred

Name? Do I read books treating of His Sacred Heart, and of His Sacred Humanity in general?

2. In my *affections.*—Do I nurture in my heart tender *love* for Jesus, doing all my actions to please Him, avoiding and detesting sin because it is displeasing to Him, trying to grow in virtue, to be more like Him?

3. In my *words.*—Do I speak of Him, of His unutterable attractiveness, gentleness, and beauty, and of His Sacred Heart, especially to children and others under my charge? Am I an *apostle* of His love, and of devotion to His Sacred Heart, and to the Blessed Sacrament?

4. In my *actions.*—Do I often visit Him and exhort others to visit Him in the Tabernacle? Do I occasionally offer up Communions and other acts of reparation to His Sacred Heart? Do I ever hear Mass for His intentions, or perform the "Stations," etc., to gain indulgences for the suffering souls dearest to His Sacred Heart?

5. In a word, do I strive to cultivate something like a *familiarity* with Jesus Christ, especially in the Blessed Eucharist?

How will Jesus Christ look upon me in the hour of death?
1. If I have been forgetful of Him and of His interests during life, how can I expect His special love of predilection at my death? With still less confidence shall I be able to stand before His Judgment Seat.

2. If, on the contrary, I have loved and served Him during life, He will console me at the hour of my death, according to the promise made to those who are devoted to His Sacred Heart. Nor shall I fear so much to stand before His dread Tribunal.

3. What, were I to die this minute! How would Jesus look upon me? Sweet Jesus, be not to me a Judge, but a Savior. Jesus! Mary! Joseph! assist me in my last agony.

VIII.—HOW THE SACRED HEART OF JESUS HAS PROVED ITS LOVE FOR US

1st Prelude.—Behold Jesus saying to you from the Cross or from the Tabernacle, "My child, I have loved thee, and delivered Myself up for love of thee " (Galatians ii. 3).

2nd Prelude. — Grace to be generous with Christ, as He has been so generous with you.

Christ has proved His love for us in three ways:

1st *Point.*—In His Incarnation.

2nd *Point.*—In His Passion and Death.

3rd *Point.*—In the Blessed Eucharist.

1st Point.—In His Incarnation.

To leave His heavenly court, that palace of ineffable bliss, where millions of adoring angels ever minister before His Throne; and, laying aside the uncreated splendors of the Godhead, to clothe Himself with our mortality; to spend nine months imprisoned in the Blessed Virgin's womb; to be born as an outcast in a stable; to live for three and thirty years in toil, sufferings, and humiliations, a life of exile on this cold, bleak earth; what greater proof, save that of giving up His life, could Jesus give us of the intense and all-consuming love for each of us that fills His Sacred Heart?

Application.—Is it possible that I believe and realize that Christ did all this for *me,* for *me* personally—to atone for my sins, to ransom *me* from everlasting slavery, and yet that I continue to offend Him; that I hesitate to make an entire and irrevocable offering of my being to His service; that I am so lukewarm, so ungenerous, so utterly forgetful of such transcendent claims upon my everlasting gratitude and love?

Affections and Resolutions.—My God and my All! Thou art all mine, and I am all Thine. Kindle Thou the all-consuming fire of Thy love within my hard, cold heart, that in an ecstasy of love I may go outside myself and see that in heaven or on earth there is nothing like to Thee.

2nd Point.—In His Passion and Death.

Consideration.—History tells us of a great and powerful king who was once most grievously offended by a vile and worthless slave. The wretched man was most deservedly condemned to death, when, lo! the monarch's only son, heir to all his vast possessions, and a prince beloved of all, and richly gifted with the rarest qualities of mind and heart, stepped forward, and insisted on giving up his life in torments at the scaffold to save the wretched criminal from the consequences of his crime. More wondrous still, the father listened to his prayer; he freed the slave and condemned his own magnanimous and unoffending son to dreadful torments and a shameful death.

Application.—We all know who is this great and powerful King, and who the generous-hearted Son who thus laid down His life to save a wretched, sin-polluted slave from death. I am this slave. What shall I do for my Deliverer? How shall I testify my gratitude?

Affections and Resolutions.—Lord, Thou hast said that no man hath greater love than this, that he give his life for his friend. Thou hast given this proof of Thy love for me; grant me grace in return to consecrate my life with all its labors, joys, and sorrows to Thy service.

3rd Point.—In the Blessed Eucharist.

Consideration.—Everything about the Blessed Eucharist breathes of love, and of self-annihilation out of love; the *end* that Jesus has in view; the *manner* of His dwelling here amongst us, the various *circumstances* that surround Him in His Eucharistic life.

The *end* is threefold: (1) To assuage the sorrows of our exile by His presence; (2) to supply us with a source of strength in our weakness, and a medicine in our spiritual maladies, by becoming the Food of our souls; (3) to expiate our sins and draw down every grace and blessing on us, by offering Himself to His Eternal Father as a Victim on our altars.

In the *manner* of His dwelling in the Tabernacle, whilst He might have gathered round Him many of the splendors of His heavenly court, He rather chooses to hide, not merely His Divinity, but even His Humanity, beneath the outward form of a little piece of bread.

What are the *circumstances* that surround him in the Eucharist? Absolute helplessness and dependence on the will of others—oftentimes poverty, neglect, and indifference; sometimes even outrage and insult. All this for my sake.

Application.—It is my sweet privilege, if I so desire, to console the Heart of Jesus in the Tabernacle. This I can do: (1) By the frequent and fervent reception of the Blessed Eucharist as an act of reparation, especially on the First Friday; (2) by hearing Mass in reparation and thanksgiving; (3) by making frequent visits to the Blessed Sacrament, especially visits of reparation; (4) by doing whatever lies in my power for the better maintenance and adornment of the Tabernacle and Altar of the Blessed Eucharist.

Affections and Resolutions.—"Lord, the zeal of Thy house hath eaten me up " (Psalm Ixviii., 10). " How lovely are Thy Tabernacles, O Lord of Hosts." (Psalm Ixxxiii., 2).

Colloquy.

Spiritual Reading: *Imitation*, Book III., chapter ii.

POINTS FOR SELF-EXAMINATION.

On Devotion to the Blessed Sacrament.

1. What *reverence* do I show to It?—(1) In my manner of genuflecting; (2) in my general behavior in the church; (3) in my manner of receiving Holy Communion; (4) do I show any mark of respect passing churches?

2. Do I give *practical proof of my devotion* to the Blessed Eucharist ?—(1) By my frequent and devout *visits* to the Blessed Sacrament; (2) by having recourse to the Tabernacle in all my joys, sorrows, doubts, and anxieties; (3) by being devout in the reception of the Blessed Eucharist, in my preparation and thanksgiving [N.B.—*(a) Remote* preparation consists in avoiding all that would displease our Lord, and in doing my daily duties well; *proximate* preparation consists in hearing Mass fervently, and exciting myself to acts of contrition, faith, desire, hope, love, etc. (b) Distinguish between sensible feelings of devotion, which, though helpful, are not necessary, and solid devotion, which consists in the firm resolution not to offend God, and the strong will to do what His service

demands from me]; (4) by hearing Mass well, and, if possible, every day; (5) by contributing, as far as in my power, towards the maintenance and adornment of the altars and churches of the Blessed Eucharist.

IX.—ON THE THINGS WHICH DISPLEASE THE SACRED HEART

1st Prelude.—Imagine Christ saying to you: "My child, cease to wound My Sacred Heart, which hath loved thee so much."

2nd Prelude.—Ask grace to get rid of whatever in you is displeasing to the Sacred Heart.

There are three things which especially displease the Sacred Heart:—

1st *Point.*—A worldly spirit.

2nd *Point.*—Tepidity in God's service.

3rd *Point.*—Sin.

1st Point.—A Worldly Spirit.

Consideration.—Even though it be your lot to live amid the cares and turmoil of the world you must not, nevertheless, be of the world. You must not belong to that world for which Christ Himself refused to pray, that world which, as He tells us, is altogether sunk in wickedness. The spirit of the world and the spirit of Christ are diametrically opposed.

The spirit of the world is the spirit of *covetousness,* which makes its highest aim to accumulate riches; the spirit of *ambition,* which at all costs seeks its own exaltation, and loves to be honored and respected by men; the spirit of *pride,* which is essentially selfish, full of self-esteem and arrogance, and looks with scorn and contempt upon the lowly.

The spirit of Christ is the spirit of *detachment* from the goods of earth, using these things as though it used them not, remembering that they are creatures subservient to a nobler and a higher end, and useful only in so far as they promote that end; it is the spirit of humility, self-sacrifice, and self-forgetfulness that toils and prays and suffers in secret, and is willing to be hid and ignored on earth.

Application.—Which of these two spirits is predominant within me? Whether I live in the world or within the sheltered haven of religion I am bound, to a greater or less degree according to my state, to banish from my heart the one and to cultivate the other.

Affections and Resolutions.—Lord, I will follow Thee whithersoever Thou goest. Grant me light and grace to know and understand the spirit of Thy Sacred Heart, that knowing It, I may love It, and loving It, I may imitate It. O Lord, make my heart like unto Thine.

2nd Point.—Tepidity in God's Service.

Consideration.—"Because thou art lukewarm, and art neither hot nor cold, I will begin to vomit thee out of My mouth" (Apocalypse iii. 16). "Cursed be he that doth the work of the Lord deceitfully" (Jeremiah xlviii. 10). These are the terrible denunciations pronounced against those who are lukewarm in God's service. God looks for much in return from those to whom He has given much.

Application.—Tepidity and real devotion to the Sacred Heart cannot exist together; one or the other must give way. Do I wish to be fervent, to shake off the spiritual languor that is apt so stealthily and silently to take possession of the soul, and secretly to undermine its strength; let me embrace *seriously* and *practically* devotion to the Sacred Heart, How am I to do so? (1) Go to Confession and Communion every First Friday. (2) Join the *Apostleship of Prayer* and get the *Decade Leaflets,* and the *Messenger* each month—they serve to keep our devotion alive. (3) Join the Sodality of the Sacred Heart, if there is one in the parish. (4) Practice the *Three Degrees* mentioned on the *Decade Leaflets.* Do these four things, and your life will be different from what it has been.

Affections and Resolutions.—Lord, enable me to realize in myself the truth of Thy promise made in favor of those who are devoted to the Sacred Heart: "*The tepid will become fervent.*"

3rd Point.—Sin.

Consideration.—Sin is God's great enemy. It has left innumerable thrones in heaven empty; it has filled the pit of hell; it is a horrid plague that desolates the earth, a hideous monster that makes eternal war on God; it is the only real evil in the world, and the source of every misery on earth.

Application.—Experience tells us we are very weak, and that the devil and our vicious nature are very strong. Of ourselves, unaided by the grace of God, we have no chance against such adversaries; but the arms are close at hand, and foremost among our weapons of defense is devotion to the Sacred Heart. It will give us courage, energy, and strength to fight the battle bravely to the end. It is our own fault, surely, if we fail to use this easy means.

Affections and Resolutions.—Lord, grant me grace to crush the serpent in my heart. O Jesus, I will rather die a thousand deaths than grievously offend and wound Thy Sacred Heart.

Colloquy.

Spiritual Reading: *Imitation,* Book III., chapter liv.

POINTS FOR SELF-EXAMINATION.

On the Spirit of the World.

We live *in* the world, but we must not be *of* the world. The Spirit of Christ is essentially opposed to the spirit of the world.

1. Christ teaches us in all things to humble ourselves and seek the lowest place; the world tells us in all ways to seek the respect and esteem of men.

2. Christ teaches us to be patient in adversity, and to forgive injuries; the world bids us to avoid and fly from suffering, in all things to gratify selflove, and to take revenge on our enemies.

3. Christ tells us that it is better to give than to receive; the world urges us to amass riches, to place our happiness in them, and to bestow as little as we can upon the poor.

4. Christ bids us to seek first the Kingdom of God and His justice; the world tells us before all things to seek the good things of this world.

5. Christ wishes us to forget ourselves and seek the good of others; the world exhorts us in everything to look to our own advantage.

6. Christ tells us to seek our happiness in the things of God; the world bids us to look for happiness in earthly things, and the indulgence of the senses.

Which are we most influenced by—the Spirit of Christ or the spirit of the world?

THE FIRST ACT OF CONSECRATION TO THE SACRED HEART OF JESUS.

COMPOSED BY BLESSED MARGARET MARY.

I *(N. N.)* give and consecrate to Thee, O Sacred Heart of our Lord Jesus Christ! my body and soul, my life, my actions, pains, and sufferings, so that I may no longer desire to employ any part of my being save in honoring, loving, and glorifying Thee. This is my irrevocable resolution—to belong entirely to Thee, and to do all for Thy love, while I renounce with my whole heart everything which could displease Thee. Wherefore, I take Thee, O Sacred Heart of Jesus! as the sole Object of my love, the Protector of my life, the Pledge of my salvation, the Remedy of my weakness and inconstancy, the Reparation for all the imperfections of my life, and my assured Refuge at the hour of my death. Be Thou, therefore, O bountiful Heart, my justification with God, Thy Heavenly Father, and turn aside from me His anger, which I have justly deserved. O Heart of Love, I place all my confidence in Thee, for I have everything to fear from my weakness, while I hope for everything from Thy bounty. Annihilate in me everything which can displease or resist Thee. Imprint Thy pure love so deeply on my heart that I may never forget Thee, nor ever be separated from Thee. I conjure Thee, by Thy infinite goodness, that my name may be engraved on Thee, since I desire to make all my happiness and all my glory consist in living and dying in quality of Thy devoted servant.

Three hundred days' Indulgence, applicable to the souls in purgatory, granted by His Holiness Leo XIII., June i, 1897.

EFFICACIOUS NOVENA TO THE SACRED HEART OF JESUS

O Divine Jesus, Who hast said: *"Ask, and you shall receive; seek, and you shall find; knock, and it shall be opened unto you,"* behold me prostrate at Thy feet. Animated with a lively faith and confidence in these promises, dictated by Thy Sacred Heart, and pronounced by Thy adorable lips, I come to ask *[here mention the request]*.

From whom shall I ask, O Sweet Jesus, if not from Thee, Whose Heart is an inexhaustible source of all graces and merits? Where shall I seek, if not in the Treasury which contains all the riches of Thy clemency and bounty? Where shall I knock, if it be not at the door of Thy Sacred Heart, through which God Himself comes to us, and through which we go to God?

To Thee, then, O Heart of Jesus, I have recourse. In Thee I find consolation when afflicted—protection when persecuted—strength when overwhelmed with trials—and light in doubt and darkness. I firmly believe Thou canst bestow on me the grace I implore, even though it should require a miracle. Thou hast only to will it, and my prayer is granted. I own

I am unworthy of Thy favors, O Jesus, but this is not a reason for me to be discouraged. Thou art the God of mercies, and Thou wilt not refuse a contrite and humble heart. Cast upon me a look of pity, I conjure Thee, and Thy compassionate Heart will find in my miseries and weakness a pressing motive for granting my petition.

But, O Sacred Heart, whatever may be Thy decision with regard to my request, I will never cease to adore, love, praise, and serve Thee. Deign, my Jesus, to accept this, my act of perfect submission to the decrees of Thy adorable Heart, which I sincerely desire may be fulfilled in and by me and all Thy creatures for ever and ever. Amen.

FORM OF CONSECRATION TO THE MOST SACRED HEART OF JESUS

Prescribed by Pope Leo XIII. on the occasion of the Consecration of the World to the Sacred Heart, June, 1899.

Most sweet Jesus, Redeemer of the human race, look down upon us, most humbly prostrate before Thine Altar. Thine we are. Thine we desire ever to remain and that we may be the more securely united to Thee, behold each one of us here to-day freely consecrates himself to Thy most Sacred Heart. Many, indeed, have never known Thee; many, too, have despised Thy commandments and rejected Thee. Have mercy on them all, O most merciful Jesus, and draw them all to Thy most Sacred Heart. Be Thou, O Lord, King, not only of the faithful who have never departed from Thee, but also of the prodigal children who have turned their backs upon Thee. Grant that they may return to their Father's house, lest they perish of wretchedness and hunger. Be Thou King of those who have been deceived by error, or whom discord keeps estranged. Bring them back to the haven of truth and to the unity of the faith, that soon there may be but one Fold and one Shepherd. Be Thou King, moreover, of all those who continue in the ancient superstitions of the Gentiles. Refuse not to deliver them out of darkness, into the light and the kingdom of God. Grant, O Lord, to Thy Church freedom and security; give peace and order to all nations; make the earth resound from pole to pole with one voice: "Praise to the Divine Heart through which our salvation has been accomplished; to the same be glory and honor for ever. Amen."

SECOND SERIES

FURTHER MEDITATIONS ON THE SACRED HEART

X.—ON THE DISPOSITIONS NECESSARY FOR DEVOTION TO THE SACRED HEART

1st Prelude. — Behold our Lord in the Tabernacle saying to you, *"Child, give Me thy heart."*

2nd Prelude. — Ask grace to understand and cultivate the dispositions necessary for acquiring true devotion to the Sacred Heart.

    1st *Point.*—First Disposition: Horror of Sin.

2nd Point.—Second Disposition: Lively Faith.

3rd Point.—Third Disposition: Real Desire to love Jesus Christ.

4th Point.—Fourth Disposition: Interior Recollection.

1st Point.—-First Disposition : Horror of Sin.

    The Sacred Heart being a fountain of infinite purity, nothing defiled can enter It. Whatever one may do to show love and honor towards It cannot be acceptable if unaccompanied by innocence of life. To the Sacred Heart sin is insupportable. It longs for the conversion of the sinner. It has graces all-sufficient to enable him to cast off sin. These graces It will give in overflowing measure, in response to prayer; but sin itself It simply loathes and will not tolerate. Hence the first essential disposition for acquiring devotion to the Sacred Heart is to cultivate great purity of soul, by keeping the soul not merely free from mortal sin, but also, as far as human frailty will suffer us, from all deliberate venial sin as well. Consider how you stand in this respect.

2nd Point.—Second Disposition : Lively Faith.

Feeble faith will never fructify into fervent love. The fundamental reason of our want of fervor in God's service is that we are lacking in a lively faith. If our faith were what it ought to be, how deep and strong and sweet would be the fervor of our love in visiting the Blessed Sacrament for instance! How the minutes and the hours, even, would fly by in that august sweet Presence, of which we never should grow weary! But because our faith is weak, we are distracted, we are restless, we are cold before the tabernacle, we are ill at ease until again we plunge into the vortex of the world of thoughtlessness without. O, what a treasure we should find in devotion to the Sacred Heart, as ever present in the tabernacle! What a solace and what strength and light we should discover in that Heart of boundless love, if we had only a more lively faith! Alas, if thou didst know the gift of God! Alas, that such priceless treasure should be hidden from us through our want of faith!

We must pray, then, for a lively faith: Lord, increase our faith. Help the weakness of our incredulity. Open the eyes of our soul that we may see; for we are blind and walking in the midst of darkness, and know nothing of the splendors of the spiritual world around us. We are like the disciples of old, "for their heart was blinded" (Mark vi. 52), and "their eyes were held that they should not know Him" (Luke xxiv. 16), till at length, in the breaking of bread, when a fuller faith was given them, "their eyes were opened and they knew Him" (Luke xxiv. 31). So, too, in the Holy Communion shall our "eyes be opened" if we pray with fervor for the gift of a lively faith.

3rd Point.—Third Disposition: Real Desire to Love Jesus Christ.

This disposition is a necessary consequence of the preceding ones, since an innocent life and a lively faith must, of necessity, lead to a great desire to love Jesus Christ. "Blessed are they," says Christ, "who hunger and thirst after justice, for they shall have their fill" (Matthew v. 6). This desire must be something more than the abstract acknowledgment on the part of our intellect of our obligation to love our Lord. Such speculative belief leads, at most, to a merely barren and useless velleity. A genuine, earnest desire is one that fills the mind; we think of it, speak of it constantly, we are ever revolving plans for its accomplishment. We never rest till we have secured what we so ardently long for. Our greatest dread is to fail in attaining it. Is our desire to love Jesus Christ a longing of this description? If not, we certainly do not "hunger and thirst after justice" We must pray, and pray often and perseveringly, for this heavenly "hunger and thirst" if we are to become truly devout to the Sacred Heart.

4th Point.—Fourth Disposition: Interior Recollection.

"Without this interior recollection it is impossible to rise towards perfection," writes Father Croiset, S.J., "and to a closer union with God, Who dwells only in peacefulness of the spirit and in the retirement of the soul freed from the entanglement of external affairs." "Whence comes it," asks another spiritual writer, "that so many pious persons, who have such good intentions, and who appear to be doing all that is necessary to make themselves saints, nevertheless get so little profit from their prayers, Communions, and reading, and after so many years' practice of all the exercises of the spiritual life, rarely show that they have at all benefited by them? How is it that their passions are still so strong, and that their defects are just what they always used to be? The only reason is their want of interior recollection." "A dissipated soul," says Croiset, "is like a lost and wandering sheep, which soon becomes a prey to the wolf. It is not easy for us, after this vagabondage, to enter into ourselves . . . the soul has lost the taste for spiritual things by too long a sojourn, as it were, in a foreign land."

Nor does this interior recollection render a man idle. On the contrary, a truly recollected and spiritual man does more real work for God than a hundred ordinary men, even though their talents be greater, perchance, than his. Witness the saints, like Francis Xavier, Francis de Sales, Ignatius, or Vincent de Paul. These men, besides maintaining a marvelous degree of interior recollection, did splendid exterior work for God. They walked in the midst of a thousand cares and distractions, yet with God ever before their eyes. Hence their success. It was not by themselves they worked; the power and strength of God was in them and worked along with them and crowned their labors with wonderful results.

Again, external occupations, however urgent or multiplied, are not necessarily a hindrance to interior recollection. The saints I have cited are proof that this constant union with God is rather promoted by the work which we do for Him, with a pure intention and under His eyes, as it were. They are so many acts and exercises of genuine love of God, for St. Ignatius tells us that love consists rather in works than in words.

XI.—ON OBSTACLES TO DEVOTION TO THE SACRED HEART

Not everyone who practices devotion to the Sacred Heart feels within himself the ardent love of God, which this devotion is so well calculated to enkindle, nor the spiritual sweetness and facility which it imparts. True, this sensible devotion, as it is termed, is not a necessary condition or a necessary constituent of sanctity; and on this ground many persons console or excuse themselves for not possessing it. Yet there is only too much reason to believe that in very many cases the loss of it is to be attributed, not to any trial or visitation of God's Providence, but to their habitual sluggishness and imperfection in God's service. The saints retained it in the midst of the severest trials. No cross or worry or affliction could deprive them of the deeply seated peace and joy of spirit that, like perennial sunshine, dwelt within their inmost soul. These precious gifts are the fruit of genuine devotion to the Sacred Heart. To enjoy them we must remove the obstacles that stand between us and such genuine devotion. These obstacles are mainly four.

1st Prelude.—Hear Christ saying to the Samaritan woman: "If thou didst know the gift of God" (John iv. 10).

2nd Prelude.—Ask grace to know and remove whatever opposes the reign of the Sacred Heart in your soul.

1st *Point.*—First obstacle to true devotion to the Sacred Heart—Tepidity.

2nd Point.—Second obstacle: Self-Love.

3rd Point.—Third obstacle: Secret Pride.

4th Point.—Fourth obstacle: Some Unmortified Passion.

1st Point.—First Obstacle to True Devotion to the Sacred Heart: Tepidity.

Devotion to the Sacred Heart necessarily implies love of our Lord. Tepidity is incompatible with such love. Therefore, as long as tepidity reigns in the soul there can be no true devotion to the Sacred Heart. Tepidity shows itself in carelessness about the commission of venial sin. The conscience ceases to take note of lesser faults. No effort is made against them. These faults become deliberate and habitual. This results in a sort of spiritual paralysis whereby the soul ceases to aim at the practice of virtue, loses its savor for prayer and self-denial, abandons the exercises of piety; faith, hope, and, above all, charity, are weakened; in a word, the fire of Divine love grows cold and is liable to become entirely extinguished under the breath of violent temptation. It is manifest that such a state of things offers an insuperable obstacle to anything like true devotion to the Sacred Heart. Nevertheless, so powerful is this devotion that, if once kindled in the soul and carefully fostered, it is capable, like the tiny spark that if nurtured gradually grows into a blazing fire, of overcoming the obstacles that bar its progress in a tepid soul, and consuming away the very elements that tend to its destruction. Hence the Promises of our Blessed Lord: "The tepid will become fervent," "the fervent will speedily rise to high perfection."

2nd Point.—Second Obstacle: Self-Love.

Self-love lies at the root of tepidity. It furnishes us with an excuse for our apathy and carelessness in serving God. It lulls the conscience with a specious appearance of virtue. It makes us think we are better than we really are. It blinds us to our sins and imperfections and brings out in bold relief before the mental vision of the soul whatever virtues or good qualities we may happen to possess. It finds a ready excuse for the neglect of prayer, in the pressure of exterior work; for the neglect of self-denial and mortification, in the plea of health. It condones its lesser faults and despises lesser virtues, on the ground that it is possessed, forsooth, of what it flatteringly terms solid virtue. It amuses itself with the vision of great deeds—to come; and has no desire to sanctify the ordinary little duties of its daily life. It lives and flourishes on self-deceit, and rests secure in its imaginary excellence. In a word, it reverses the Gospel precept of looking on ourselves in all things as unprofitable servants.

3rd Point.—Third Obstacle: Secret Pride.

Closely allied to self-love is secret pride. It is the mother no less of presumption than of the excessive depression and discouragement that are so great a hindrance to perseverance. It attacks the motives of our actions. We fancy it is God's glory we are seeking, when in reality it is nothing but our personal glory or aggrandizement we have at heart. Hence our keen appreciation of the honor and applause we get. Hence our over exaltation in success, our over-depression and discouragement in failure. Hence, too, the secret vexation at another's good success, the susceptibilities, the estrangements, the petty jealousy and all the brood of low, unworthy thoughts and words and acts that make us feel ashamed at times of the poor, weak human nature that is in us. It is clear that this vice is profoundly opposed to the reign of the Sacred Heart within our souls. Humility, the unreserved surrender of the world's esteem, of self and all that flatters self, is the first and most necessary condition of the establishment of the reign of Christ within us.

4th Point.—Fourth Obstacle: Some Unmortified Passion.

There is always someone passion or disordered inclination that is ever rising in rebellion. It lurks within the heart like a traitor in the citadel, ever ready to throw open the gates and betray the stronghold to the enemy. The worst of it is that, so far from dealing with it summarily and treating it as a most dangerous foe, we temporize with it and flatter it. War to the knife, relentless, persevering war, is the only remedy for this disorder. It matters little that the other enemies are crushed. A leak may sink a ship, a tiny crack brings down the noblest edifice, a spark produces a mighty conflagration. One single unmortified passion is enough to overthrow the kingdom of the Sacred Heart within the soul.

Here, then, are the four great obstacles to true devotion to the Sacred Heart. In the next meditation we shall see what means we must adopt to overcome them.

XII.—ON MEANS OF ACQUIRING DEVOTION TO THE SACRED HEART

In the last meditation we reflected on the chief obstacles to devotion to the Sacred Heart. We shall now consider some of the chief means by which we may acquire this devotion; in other words, by which we may increase in the love of our Lord's Divine Heart.

1st Prelude. — Behold Christ in the Blessed Sacrament interceding for the salvation of men.

2nd Prelude.—Ask grace to put in practice the means of acquiring devotion to the Sacred Heart.

1st *Point.*—First Means: Prayer.

2nd Point.—Second Means: Devotion to the Blessed Sacrament.

3rd Point.—Third Means: Devotion to the Blessed Virgin.

4th Point.—Fourth Means: Fidelity to the Practices of the Devotion.

1st Point. — First Means: Prayer (First Degree of the Apostleship of Prayer).

Prayer is the universal and all-powerful means of getting everything we want from God. Sometimes, indeed, it happens that we pray, and pray earnestly, yet we do not seem to receive any answer. This may happen either because God sees that what we so earnestly desire is not really what is best for us, and in this case He gives us something else instead, that He knows to be more for our real good; or else it may be that He keeps back the boon we ask for, either to test our constancy and then bestow it on us in still fuller measure, or even keeps it over for some future time when we shall stand more urgently in need of it, possibly even reserving it for the supreme moment of our death. But there is one grace He is always anxious to give us at once and in the fullest degree, and that is the grace to love Him and to be devoted to His Sacred Heart. We may always be assured that Christ will grant our prayers abundantly and promptly when we ask Him for the grace to know and love His Sacred Heart. In the "Morning Offering" of the First Degree of the Apostleship of Prayer, we offer all our daily actions as constant prayer to God, to grant us this and other favors.

Thou, O Lord, Who didst come to cast fire upon earth, vouchsafe to cast into my heart the burning fire of Thy love. I offer to Thee, unreservedly and forever, this poor cold heart of mine. Inflame it, set it all on fire with Thy love. Its every throb shall henceforth be an ardent act of love of Thee. May it find no rest, no happiness, no joy, outside of Thee. May it live for Thee and love Thee *alone,* both now and through the endless ages of eternity. Amen.

2nd Point.—Second Means: Devotion to the Blessed Sacrament (Third Degree).

Devotion to the Blessed Sacrament goes hand in hand with devotion to the Sacred Heart and is a sovereignly efficacious means of acquiring it. Devotion to the Blessed Sacrament exists under three distinct aspects:

(1) The *Mass.* The infinite Sacrifice of the Mass is obviously a *most* powerful means of acquiring devotion to the Sacred Heart. It is the oblation of the Sacred Heart to the Eternal Father, whereby we may with certainty impetrate from God the grace of deep and tender love of His Divine Son.

(2) *Communion.* Here we approach and receive the Sacred Heart within us. "Can a man hide fire in his bosom . . . and not burn?" asks Solomon (Proverbs vi. 27). "Divine love," says Father Croiset, S.J., "has kindled, as it were, a furnace upon our altars in the adorable Eucharist, and it is by drawing near to this sacred flame that all the saints have been set on fire with a love, most ardent and profound, for Jesus Christ." "Your principal intention in communicating," says St. Francis de Sales, "should be to make progress and gain strength in the love of God."

(3) *Visits to the Blessed Sacrament.* "Among men," says Father Croiset, "friendship is maintained and drawn closer by frequent visits and conversations. By the same means, also, is it that we learn to have a more ardent love for Jesus Christ." It is, often, in moments spent before the lonely tabernacle that our Lord makes His voice heard in the silence of our souls and teaches us the secrets of His Sacred Heart. At such times, perhaps, more than at any other, Christ converses familiarly with His friends, communicates to them the treasures of His Heart, and sets their souls aglow with His Divine love. In the Third Degree of the Apostleship of Prayer, frequent Communion is urged upon us; and frequent Communion implies frequent hearing of Mass and frequent visits to the Blessed Sacrament.

Enable me, O Lord, to use diligently and perseveringly these three great means of growing in devotion to Thy Sacred Heart. In daily Mass, in daily Communion, in daily Visits to the Blessed Sacrament, I shall ever find most powerful incentives to devotion to Thy Divine Heart.

3rd Point.—Third Means: Devotion to the Blessed Virgin (Second Degree).

Our Blessed Lady is "the Mother of fair love" (Ecclesiasticus xxiv. 24). To her we should have recourse to acquire an ardent love for the Sacred Heart. "Jesus Christ," says St. Bernard, "readily grants to her what we are unworthy to receive." She is the channel of His graces, the dispenser of His gifts. And no grace or no gift will she more readily procure for us than that of a deep and tender devotion to the Sacred Heart of her Divine Son. It is for this reason that in the Second Degree, as it is termed, of the Apostleship of Prayer, we turn to Mary, invoking her assistance through the *Pater* and ten *Aves* we address to her; and that in the First Degree we offer all our actions, etc., through her hands to God.

4th Point.—Fourth Means: Fidelity to the Practices of Devotion to the Sacred Heart.

These practices are systematized and organized into a consistent and coherent whole in the exercises of the Apostleship of Prayer, which is a world-wide league or organization of devotion to the Sacred Heart, embracing in its ranks some twenty-five million of clients of the Sacred Heart the wide world over. Its three main practices are termed the "Three Degrees," which, as we have seen, embrace the principal exercises of devotion to the Sacred Heart. To these are annexed many subsidiary exercises, such as the "Holy Hour," the "Guard of Honor," the "Nine Offices," and so forth, all of which are but phases, so to speak, of the exercises practiced in the "Three Degrees."

XIII.—ON THE LOVE OF THE SACRED HEART FOR US—OUR INGRATITUDE TOWARDS IT

1st Prelude. — Imagine Christ in the Blessed Sacrament appearing to Blessed Margaret Mary and showing her His Heart, pierced in the side, crowned with thorns, surmounted by a cross and with flames bursting forth from within: the symbols of His love and of His sufferings for ungrateful man.

2nd Prelude. — Beg for grace to understand in some degree the excessive love of the Sacred Heart for mankind, on the one hand, and on the other, the amazing ingratitude of men.

1st *Point.*—The excessive Love of the Sacred Heart for Men.

2nd Point.—The amazing Ingratitude of Men towards the Sacred Heart.

3rd Point.—The Feelings of the Sacred Heart with regard to this Ingratitude.

1st Point.—The Excessive Love of the Sacred Heart for Men.

Christ is God. His Heart is a Divine Heart. It burns with a love that is Divine, a love that can be measured by no human standard, that utterly transcends the farthest reach of our poor human understanding, a love that, like all else in God, is infinite, unbounded, unimaginable.

We seem at times to get a faint and far-off glimpse into that fathomless abyss of love—to peer into the depths that make us dizzy as we gaze, just as persons creeping cautiously to the very brink of a volcano look into the profound abyss with awesome wonder and shrink back overwhelmed at the mere sight of the limitless expanse that glows beneath.

Truly you have only to consult your own experience. What a world of love the Heart of Christ has expended—shall I call it wasted?— upon each of us! In spite of utter coldness, waywardness and sin, in spite of positive resistance to His inspirations, has He not pursued you till, in a manner, He well-nigh forced you to capitulate to His relentless love?

2nd Point.—The amazing Ingratitude of Men towards the Sacred Heart.

Just think how many there are, out of the vast population of the world at this present moment, who are utterly ignorant of God and His love, who know nothing of the marvel of His Life and bitter Passion and Death, or of His wonderful existence in the Blessed Eucharist. They neither know nor care. And yet they are His creatures, and He died for them, and fain would bring them to the everlasting fellowship of the angelic hosts.

But worse than this remains. Of those who know Him and the wonders of His never-ending love, how few there are that show even the faintest appreciation of His boundless goodness—how many that entirely ignore it!

Then leaving out of view the great, the overwhelming majority of human beings, what is the conduct of the chosen few who call themselves the servants of the Sacred Heart? Is there anyone amongst them all who renders Him a tithe of the devotion and the love that He deserves? Question your own soul and ask yourself: "What has He done for me, and what have I done for Him in return? Would I venture to treat the humblest of my fellow beings as I have treated Him?"

3rd Point.—The Feelings of the Sacred Heart with Regard to this Ingratitude.

Jesus Christ is Man as well as God. He has the feelings and the sensitiveness of a man, refined indeed to a supreme degree, yet human just as much as yours and mine. If an ordinary fellow being had done a hundredth part of what our Lord has done for you, and you had treated him in anything at all approaching to the way in which you treat the Sacred Heart, what, I ask, would be his feelings? God cast off the guilty Jews to wander blindly in their black ingratitude. What charity, what patience, what long suffering He has shown in your regard!

He has, indeed, on some occasions, given vent to the bitter feelings of His wounded Heart of love. From the secret silence of the tabernacle He has spoken, now and then, to chosen souls; as when He said to Blessed Margaret Mary: "Ah, this is a greater torment to Me than any that I suffered in My Passion. If men did but render to Me love for love, I should count as nothing all that I have done for them. I would willingly do even more, if it were possible; but the desire that I have to benefit them meets with no return but coldness and repulse!" "What affects Me most," He added on another occasion, "is that I am treated so by hearts that are consecrated to Me."

Today, nay, every day throughout the entire year, especially on the Feast of His Most Sacred Heart, He fain would win from you the generous tribute of your *gratitude* and *reparation*. Oh, what will He not do for one who strives with earnest, loving mind to offer Him this twofold tribute He so longs for; for him who strives to lessen the bitterness of the lament: "I looked for one that would grieve together with Me *and there was none,* and for one that would comfort Me *and I found none*" (Psalm lxviii. 21).

Resolutions.—(1) Frequently to offer the Mass at which you assist as an infinite sacrifice of gratitude and reparation to the Sacred Heart. (2) In your Communions to make to the Sacred Heart an unreserved oblation of your whole being for the same intentions. (3) Now and then throughout the day to offer all the Masses then being said throughout the world for these same intentions. (4) To make a visit of thanksgiving and reparation daily to the tabernacle.

XIV.—ON THE INCOMPARABLE MAJESTY AND GREATNESS OF THE SACRED HEART

1st Prelude. — Behold Jesus Christ revealing His Sacred Heart to Blessed Margaret Mary.

2nd Prelude.—Ask grace to understand the incomparable majesty and greatness of the Sacred Heart, and to be animated with becoming sentiments of love and veneration in Its regard.

    1st Point.—The Sacred Heart is united with the Divinity of the Eternal Word.

2nd Point.—The Sacred Heart is the Seat and Centre of the love of Christ.

3rd Point.—The Sacred Heart is the Victim of our sins, in the Redeemer's Passion and Death and in the Eucharist.

 1st Point.—The Sacred Heart is United with the Divinity of the Eternal Word.

The Divine Nature was united not merely to the Soul, but to the Body of Jesus Christ. His Heart is, therefore, a Divine Heart, the Heart of God Himself. To say this is to say all that can be said about the Sacred Heart. It is to place It before us as a Heart of incomparable majesty and greatness, calling for the profoundest homage, love, and veneration we are capable of rendering It.

How sublimely great, therefore, are the treasures that enrich the Sacred Heart! Our mind cannot conceive them, because no mortal mind can grasp the majesty, the purity, the sanctity of God. This Royal Heart is mighty with the strength and majesty of God Himself. This Heart is holy with the holiness of God Himself. This Heart is sweet and generous and lovable and faithful with the sweetness and the generosity, the love and the fidelity, of God Himself. Oh, now, perhaps for the first time, I begin to have some faint idea of the priceless value of the Sacred Heart. O my Divine Savior, make my wretched heart a little less unworthy of Thee. O Heart of my Redeemer, noble, faithful, generous, and loving, beyond the utmost reach of my imagination, take complete possession of this poor, cold, sinful heart of mine.

What a difference between my heart and that of Christ! Yet all the treasures of His Heart are at my disposal, to make up for the almost entire lack of every virtue and good quality that I find within my own. I will borrow of Its sanctity to make up for all my sinfulness. I will clothe myself with its surpassing strength to fortify my weakness. Its wisdom and its light shall chase away the darkness of my earthly heart. My heart, so often sorrowful and crushed beneath the trials of this life, shall find a supernatural courage and happiness and peace in Thee, O Sacred Heart of my Redeemer!

2nd Point.—The Sacred Heart the Seat and Centre of the Love of Christ.

In our human way of speaking, we attribute to the *heart* the qualities that we admire in the *person:* we say a person is kind-hearted, noble-hearted, generous-hearted, and so on. Of all human passions and emotions that register their workings on the heart of man none affect it so profoundly as does love. Hence in man the heart is taken as the special seat of love. Now Jesus Christ is truly Man, therefore is His Heart the human seat and center of His love.

Jesus showed His Heart to Blessed Margaret Mary, with flames bursting forth from within, to show that His Heart is a very furnace of Divine love, the focus of that all-consuming fire of love that motived all His actions from Bethlehem to Calvary, that keeps Him a willing Victim on our altars and a loving Prisoner in our tabernacles. The secret history of that love is written in His wounded Hands and Feet and Side, and still more in the wondrous mystery of the Eucharist.

And *you have cost that Divine yet Human Heart so many pangs;* you have been the object of its sweet yet ardent transports. It has thought of you and loved you from the first, and with an intensity of love that neither human lips can tell, nor mind conceive. Should you not be His, and His *alone,* for evermore? Should not the one great business of your life, henceforth, be to live for Him and love Him with all the fervor and intensity of your entire being?

3rd Point.—The Sacred Heart the Victim of Sin.

1. The heart is the seat of grief as well as of love —the grief that springs from unrequited love. The Heart of Christ was rent and torn with the unseen martyrdom of love before the soldier's hand had pierced It on the cross. The fear, the weariness, the sadness that assailed It in the Garden, the awful vision of the sins of men, from which It shrank with such unutterable loathing, Its foreknowledge of the black ingratitude of future ages —all this was its martyrdom beneath the olives of Gethsemani.

2. Another martyrdom awaited It within the silent tabernacle. Infinitely and imperturbably happy, yet here, too, in a mysterious manner, that great human Heart of Christ upon the altar, glowing with the ardors of an infinite yet unrequited love of man, waits and longs and mourns for some small recognition of Its love.

3. And shall not *I,* at least, endeavor in my own poor way to satisfy the longings of this Heart of love? I have grieved and wounded It in days gone by. With what a wondrous love and patience It has borne with me, waited for me, drawn me back from the abyss! But now and henceforth, my one great aim and effort is, and ever shall be, to make my Benefactor known and loved by men as He deserves, and by my love and service to endeavor to atone in some degree for all the utter coldness and indifference by which my Savior's Heart is wounded in His own sweet Sacrament of Love.

XV.—ON THE HIDDEN LIFE OF THE SACRED HEART IN THE BLESSED EUCHARIST

1st Prelude.—Fancy yourself alone with Jesus in the desert, or in the Tabernacle.

2nd Prelude.—Ask grace to understand the *nature* and *advantages* of this hidden life.

1st *Point.*—Nature of this Hidden Life.

2nd *Point.*—Advantages of this Hidden Life.

1st Point.—Nature of this Hidden Life.

Look at the Tabernacle! What silence, solitude, humility, absence of all that could attract the senses reigns there! Yet faith tells you that it is God Himself—the God Who moves and governs the universe, Who guides the courses of the stars, and watches over men and angels—He it is Who dwells in everlasting silence there behind the little door! He tells you here of the *internal spirit* that should be the animating principle of your interior life. He presents to you a *model* for your imitation. In all your actions you should look to God, and seek to please Him only, and to do His holy Will. The world seeks the blaze of notoriety, it courts applause, and lives its fevered life amid the noise and rush and hurry of exterior things. The silent, lonely Dweller in the Tabernacle is infinitely happy in His humble, narrow home. Calmly, noiselessly, and yet omnipotently, He is exercising a supremely marvelous apostolate, whose operations are infinite in their extent and variety. He rules the world, and the world knows Him not. His life is one of everlasting prayer, and union with His Heavenly Father, and obedience, and submission to His Will. Within such narrow limits He is giving us, His creatures, the most sublime example of all virtues.

2nd Point.—Advantages of this Hidden Life.

1. *It serves to disengage us from the world and from ourselves. Deafened* and distracted by the jar of earthly interests, we can never *hear* the still, small voice of conscience urging us to better things, or hearken to the secret inspirations of God's grace. *Blinded* by the glare and glitter of the world, we can never *see* aright the things of God, or follow up the path that leads to heaven. Nay, like those wandering lights that guide the traveler, night bound on the treacherous morass, to his destruction, the allurements of the worldly objects that attract the senses draw us speedily and surely to destruction. It is only by withdrawing from this outer darkness of the world and keeping in the light of sanctifying grace that we can hope to reach our everlasting home in safety.

2. *This hidden life secures the peace and quiet of the soul.* The roar and turmoil of the world is inimical to our salvation. The ship that sails on stormy waters is in danger of being wrecked and may never reach the port. The passions are the storms that wreck the soul. Within the quiet shelter of the hidden life their violence is checked, and they are held in sway.

3. *The hidden life promotes the spirit of prayer.* Amid the countless dissipations and frivolities of worldly life it is impossible to live the life of prayer. Within the sheltering haven of the hidden life prayer becomes natural and easy. It is the very atmosphere of one's surroundings, the breath and nourishment of the interior life.

4. *The hidden life is full of sweetness, fostered by the choicest gifts of heaven.* The votaries of worldly pleasure often find it bitter to the taste. Like Dead Sea fruits that "tempt the eye, all bitterness within," the pleasures and enjoyments of this life are often sadly disappointing. On the other hand, the pure, serene

enjoyments of the hidden life of grace are true and solid. Melancholy is a thing that is unknown to the interior soul. It has, no doubt, its sorrows and its trials, but, like the winds that sweep the ocean, they merely touch the surface, and leave the depths below unruffled and at peace.

Resolution.—In your visits to the Blessed Sacrament ask the Sacred Heart to teach you how to enter on this hidden life, of which He gives you such a wonderful example.

Aspiration.— "In peace, in the selfsame, I will sleep and I will rest " (Psalm iv. 9).

XVI.—ON THE ACTIVE LIFE OF THE SACRED HEART IN THE BLESSED EUCHARIST

What a marvelous activity there is within that lonely, silent Tabernacle! It is the busiest spot on earth. For thence, though with none of the rush and roar of the busy world without, the Prisoner of Love, apparently so helpless and so abandoned, is all the while ruling with omnipotent hand the material universe, shaping the destinies of men, guiding, guarding, watching over the myriad interests of immortal souls.

1st Prelude.—Imagine you behold the Sacred Heart in the Tabernacle, occupied with all the interests of the vast universe of mind and matter.

2nd Prelude.—Ask grace to imitate the zeal of the Sacred Heart and Its manner of exercising that zeal.

1st *Point.*—The Occupations of the Sacred Heart in the Tabernacle.

2nd Point.—The Manner in which the Sacred Heart acts in the Eucharist.

1st Point.—The Occupations of the Sacred Heart in the Tabernacle.

1. What is the Sacred Heart ever occupied with in the Tabernacle? (1) From that Tabernacle He is directing and watching over the general interests of the Church. "Behold I am with you all days, even to the consummation of the world." Amid the storms that rage so fiercely round the Bark of Peter and seem to threaten its destruction, Christ is ever in the midst of His afflicted children, even as of old upon the Sea of Galilee He was with His Apostles in the tempest. And just as then He seemed to sleep, unconscious of their peril, so, within the Tabernacle, does He seem to worldly men to be unconscious of the strife that surges round the Church. "I sleep and My Heart watcheth" (Canticles v. 2). To the eye of faith the great Heart of Christ is ever "watching" from the altar over the safety of the Church. At the crisis of its sorrow He will rise and "bid the winds be still," and "there will follow a great calm." (2) And who can tell the wondrous operations of the Eucharistic Heart in individual souls? He instructs the ignorant, He comforts the afflicted, He reproves the wayward, He calls the sinner to repentance, and urges on the just to greater holiness. He fortifies the weak, and with His Sacraments supports them in their every need. Every moment of the day and night He offers Himself up as an infinite and priceless Sacrifice to draw down every blessing on His creatures. From the newly-born infant at the font of Baptism to the dying sinner in his agony, *all* become participators in the boundless mercy of the Sacred Heart.

2. We must, in our own measure, strive to imitate the active life of Jesus in the Tabernacle. We should endeavor to promote His interests, not in a languid and sleepy way, but with all the energy of our whole mind and body. Surely this is the least that we may do for Him in return for all that He has done for us. Work and toil as we may for Him, we can never hope to repay Him a thousandth part of what we owe Him. To make an entire and unreserved oblation of our whole being and of all our energies of soul and body to His service is but giving Him what is already on a thousand titles His. What greater privilege or happiness could you desire than to spend yourself to your last breath in working for Him? Henceforth let His interests be yours. Let all that concerns Him concern you. Consider no sacrifice too great, no effort too prolonged, to show your love for Him and your desire to advance His glory.

2nd Point.—The Manner in which the Sacred Heart acts in the Blessed Eucharist.

1. The active life of the Sacred Heart in the Blessed Eucharist is the model of the active life that we should strive to lead. It is a life of *prayer,* a life of closest *union* with His Heavenly Father. There is no noise or hurry of outward act, no inordinate attachment to exterior work, no bustle or rush of feverish impetuosity. All is calm, peaceful, prayerful, recollected. With the gentle, patient sweetness of omnipotent love, the Sacred Heart insinuates His powerful graces into souls, as warm sunshine penetrates into a room, bringing with it all the joy and brightness of the summer sun. And so the prayerful, kindly spirit scatters round it the joyous sunshine of God's love. Its very presence is a magnetic influence attracting other souls to God. It dwells in an atmosphere of prayer, and the strength and grace and sweetness of the Sacred Heart are with it in its every work for God.

2. The life of Jesus in the Blessed Eucharist is also a life of wonderful *examples.* He gives us a marvelous example of humility, of self-sacrifice, or, rather, self-effacement; of mortification, of detachment from the things of earth, of prayer, obedience, zeal. His presence in the Tabernacle is a perpetual exhortation to us to try and imitate Him in these virtues. He is ever, by the power of example, preaching silent sermons of surpassing eloquence.

In this, too, we can imitate Him. In our daily lives we may, even though unconsciously, be ever drawing souls to God by the silent living eloquence of good example.

XVII.—ON THE SACRED HEART AS A FOUNTAIN OF GRACE IN THE BLESSED EUCHARIST

1st Prelude. — Imagine Jesus in the Blessed Sacra¬ment showing you His Sacred Heart, from which there flows a stream of crystal water, to denote the graces He so longs to pour into your soul.

2nd Prelude. — Stand before Him as a poor leper, languishing with thirst, and beg Him to cleanse and cure and vivify your fainting soul.

1st Point.—The Sentiments of the Sacred Heart in our regard.

2nd Point.—The Sentiments the Sacred Heart desires to find in us.

1st Point.—The Sentiments of the Sacred Heart in our regard.

1. What were His sentiments during His mortal life? We are told "He went about on all sides doing good and curing all." He gave speech to the dumb, hearing to the deaf, sight to the blind. The sick came to Him in crowds to be cured of

their corporal maladies. While curing their bodies, He conferred spiritual health upon their souls. Does He not do the very same today? We never open a copy of the Messenger without finding in it a long and varied record of the many favors granted by His Sacred Heart to those who call on Him for help. There are thanksgivings for spiritual favors: for conversions to the faith or from a life of sin, for the grace that emancipates the drunkard from the slavery of drink, or brings back the erring child a prodigal, repentant, to his father's home. There are thanksgivings for temporal favors: for broken health restored, for means of livelihood procured, for peace in families, and plenty granted to the frugal board. Is it not as true to say today as when He lived in visible form amongst us that "He goes about on all sides doing good and curing all"?

2. His Heart is a furnace glowing fiercely in the very ardor of Its longing to communicate Itself to men. It experiences a sort of inexpressible suffering from the excess of graces It contains, looking, as it does, oftentimes in vain, for someone to receive them. "My Heart can no longer support Its desire to communicate Itself to souls," He once said to Blessed Margaret Mary, "do thou assist Me to lessen the pain. Publish and cause it to be published all over the world that I will set no limits to My graces for those souls that come to seek them in My Heart."

3. And nevertheless you are so distrustful, so reserved in your dealings with the Sacred Heart. Why have you hitherto received so little? Because you did not go to Him with sufficient confidence and love. O Heart of infinite liberality, when shall I learn to know Thee, to love Thee and to trust Thee as I ought?

2nd Point.—The Sentiments the Sacred Heart desires to find in us

1. You should turn to the Sacred Heart in every need. There is balm for every wound, light for every doubt, succor in distress, help for every need, a cure for every sickness, in the Sacred Heart. Why is it that you go everywhere else before you turn to Him Whose power is omnipotent and Whose love is boundless? "Come to Me all you that labor and are heavy burdened, and I will refresh you." He is waiting, waiting patiently, for you to come.

2. You should go to Him with a sincere and strong desire for the graces that you need. Half-hearted velleities, well-nigh smothered by a secret misgiving that your

prayers will not be heard, are little better than an insult to the Sacred Heart. In order to receive His graces, you must be sincere and in earnest with our Lord.

3. Lastly, you must go to Him with humble, loving confidence. He allows you to act towards Him with an affectionate familiarity. You some¬times admit some fellow-creature, weak and sinful like yourself, to the closest confidence. You tell your secrets to that person, or you turn to him for guidance and advice. Later on he may betray your trust, or else turn away from or forget you. The Divine Heart of Christ, infinitely amiable and true and loving, will never abandon or be false to you.

Colloquy.—Open your whole heart to the Sacred Heart of Jesus. Consecrate yourself to Jesus Christ unreservedly and forever. Disclose to Him your hopes and fears and wishes. Place your salvation in His Hands.

XVIII.—ON THE LIFE OF LOVE OF THE SACRED HEART IN THE BLESSED EUCHARIST

The wonderful Life of Love which the Sacred Heart of Jesus lives in the Blessed Sacrament of the Altar ought often to be the subject of our thoughts, especially during the month of the Sacred Heart. This love is exemplified, especially, in the fact that *He is always and everywhere with us* as our *Companion,* our *Sacrifice,* our *Food.*

1st Prelude.—Fix your eyes on the Tabernacle. Make a lively act of faith in His real living *presence* there. Hear Him address to you the words: "Behold, I am with you all days, even to the consummation of the world."

2nd Prelude.—Ask grace to understand the wondrous love of the Sacred Heart for you in the Blessed Eucharist, and to show your deep gratitude in return.

1st Point.—The Sacred Heart the Companion of our exile in the Blessed Eucharist.

2nd Point.—The Sacred Heart a loving Victim in the Blessed Eucharist.

3rd Point.—The Sacred Heart the Food of our souls in the Blessed Eucharist.

1st Point.—The Sacred Heart the Companion of our Exile in the Blessed Eucharist.

"My delights," He tells us through the Wise Man, "are to be with the children of men." By a miracle of His Omnipotence, He multiplies His presence all the world over. Even though it exposes Him to innumerable insults from His enemies, and neglect and coldness from His friends, He would fain be ever in our midst. How patiently He waits for us to come to Him! Throughout the long hours of the day, when men, with scarce a thought about the lonely Prisoner of the Tabernacle, are hurrying past Him in the noisy streets of the big city; in the dark, silent watches of the night, when the world around is buried in unconscious sleep, that Heart, so full of love, is ever watching, waiting, praying, in the Tabernacle, When the dawn returns, brightening on the hill-tops, a faithful few —how very few!—come in to visit Him, and assist at the daily sacrifice of the Mass. Throughout the day He is practically left alone. Yet how He longs for some to come and speak to Him, and keep Him company, and tell Him of their wants, their sorrows, and their hopes! "Come to Me," He says, "all you that labor and are burdened, and I will refresh you " (Matthew xi. 28).

2nd Point.—The Sacred Heart a Loving Victim in the Blessed Eucharist.

What a treasure, what a marvel, is the Mass! It is a daily renewal of the Sacrifice of Calvary: "Of equal value," says St. Chrysostom, "with the Sacrifice of the Cross"; " There is nothing in holy Church so sublime and of such inestimable value," says Osorius;" It is the sum of all spiritual exercises, the mainspring of devotion, the soul of piety, the fire of Divine charity, the abyss of Divine mercy and a precious means whereby God confers on us His graces," says St. Francis de Sales. And yet, though there is nothing so helpful to save and sanctify our souls, nothing that gives such pleasure and such glory to the Sacred Heart, how few of us there are, despite the fact that we might so easily do so, who make a point to assist at *daily Mass!* Shall we not resolve to sanctify at least the month of June by trying to hear Mass *each day* in honor of the Sacred Heart.

3rd Point.—The Sacred Heart the Food of our Souls in the Blessed Eucharist.

What a wonderful *excess of love* that Jesus should condescend, not merely to dwell in our midst in the Tabernacle, and be our daily Sacrifice upon the Altar, but that He should actually become our Food! No mind of man can fully grasp, no tongue can adequately tell of such a marvel. Not merely once a year, or once a month, but every week, nay, every day, our Blessed Savior invites us to this heavenly banquet. Priceless and innumerable are the treasures that await us there. And yet how few there are that give this pleasure to the Sacred Heart of coming to the banquet daily! How it would inflame our hearts with love to do so!

Resolutions. — To hear Mass and to go to Communion very often—if possible each day—this month, in honor of the Sacred Heart. To pray that daily Mass and daily Communion may, as the Sovereign Pontiff wishes, become more and more in practice among the clients of the Sacred Heart.

THIRD SERIES

THE APOSTLESHIP OF PRAYER

INTRODUCTION

Its Nature

The Apostleship of Prayer is a League of prayer and zeal in union with the Sacred Heart of Jesus, embracing in its ranks some twenty-five million people of all nations. It is styled *Apostleship*, because its members are *apostles* banded together to promote the interests of the Sacred Heart and the salvation of souls. It is styled Apostleship of *Prayer*, because the great means it employs to secure its object is prayer. (See Meditations XIX., XXL, XXIII., etc.) One of its chief exercises is what is termed the *Morning Offering* or daily morning oblation of all the thoughts, words, actions, and sufferings of the day, for the intentions of the Sacred Heart. (See Meditations XXV. and XXVI.) Moreover, it is an Apostleship of Prayer *in union with the Sacred Heart of Jesus*, because in all that it does and offers it acts in union with the Heart of Christ, making His interests and intentions its own, and by virtue of the strength and power it possesses therefrom, and from its intimate participation in the merits and grace of the Redeemer, increasing in a marvelous degree the value and efficacy of its own endeavors. It is obvious that such an expression of devotion is eminently Catholic and fruitful of sanctification, both in the souls of those who practice it, and of those on whose behalf its practices are offered.

Its Practice

Chief among the practices of the Apostleship of Prayer are what are called "The Three Degrees." (See Meditation XXV.)

The *first,* which alone is essential to participation in the work, consists in the making of "The Morning Offering." (See Meditation XXVI.)

The *second* consists in offering daily a *Pater* and ten *Aves* to the Blessed Virgin for the intentions of the Apostleship. (See Meditation XXV., 2nd Point.) This practice itself imports a considerable amount of vocal prayer into one's daily life, and fosters devotion to our Blessed Lady.

The *third* demands a monthly or weekly communion of reparation *in turn* from the members, thus carrying out the well-known injunction laid on Blessed Margaret Mary by our Lord Himself. Some 60,000,000 Communions are thus offered yearly by the members of this Third Degree. In view of the recent legislation of the Church it is not easy to overestimate the value of this practice in promoting the frequent reception of the Blessed Eucharist.

To pass from one "Degree" to another, no formality is requisite. Special and very large indulgences are attached to the practice of each of these "Degrees."

Its Spirit

The salvation of souls was the object of the Incarnation of the Son of God, the motive that impelled the Savior of the world to labor, to suffer and to die, and furthermore to bestow on us the crowning gift of the Blessed Eucharist. In spite of all that He has done for them, many souls have been, and will be, lost forever. The Redeemer as He lay in agony beneath the olives in the garden must have felt the bitterness of the lament uttered by the Royal Prophet in the Psalms, *What profit is there in my blood*? (Psalm xxix. 10). His Sacred Heart, all bruised and bleeding under the appalling weight of sin that forced Its very Blood, like sweat, to ooze in ruddy streams through every pore, must longingly have looked adown the ages yet to come for those that would espouse His cause, and by their prayers and sufferings and good works, in union with His own, make fruitful in the souls so precious in the sight of God the dearly purchased graces of redemption.

This is the central thought of the Apostleship of Prayer, the very essence of its spirit, to become the champions and apostles of the love of Christ, as manifested in His Sacred Heart, and make His labors, death, and sufferings fruitful for the saving of the souls of sinful men.

Its History

The modest foundations of the now world-wide Association of the Apostleship of Prayer were laid in 1844 by Father Gautrelet, S. J., in the College of Puy, in the south of France. From this it spread abroad with wonderful and ever-increasing rapidity, till now it numbers some 25,000,000 associates. In 1849 it was enriched by Pius IX. with many indulgences. Pope Leo XIII., while yet a bishop, said of it: *"The Apostleship of Prayer is so beautiful a work and unites so much fruitfulness with so much simplicity, that it assuredly deserves all the favor of ecclesiastical authority. I rejoice to see it established in my diocese, and I shall never tire of promoting it."* And in a pastoral letter of 1868 he says: *"The plentiful fruit which the Holy League has already produced, no less than its rapid extension, shows plainly how pleasing this association must be to our Lord."*

But it was only later on, as Pope, that Leo XIII. gave full expression to the warmth of his approval. In 1879 he drew up special statutes for the Apostleship, thus to perfect and define its scope and organization. In no less than eight successive Briefs or Rescripts, each conferring some new grace or privilege, the Holy Father marked his warm appreciation of the fruits and labors of the League and raised it to its present perfect state.

Within the last thirty years the development of the Association has been marvelous. It is still spreading far and wide throughout the Church, and is, each day, bringing forth fresh fruits of sanctity and zeal. It has now some 67,238 aggregated centers, with forty-two *Messengers,* published in twenty-seven languages.

Such rapid and extraordinary development, coupled with the simplicity of its organization and the abundant graces that the Sacred Heart has so manifestly poured upon it, mark out this world-wide crusade of prayer as a most powerful instrument raised up by Providence for the succor of the Church in these latter days of coldness and infidelity.

Its Organization

The Apostleship of Prayer is divided into what are termed "Centers". The Center consists of a local Director, Promoters, and Members. Any parish, convent, institute, or school may become an affiliated Centre on applying to the *Messenger* Office of the country in question. The members are divided into groups of fifteen or thirty, called "Circles," each under the charge of a Promoter. The Promoters are the officers of the League.

N.B.—Full instructions for establishing the Apostleship are sent on the application of priests and superiors of institutions to the *Messenger* Office, Roehampton, London; Great Denmark Street, Dublin; 801 W. 181st Street, New York; St. Patrick's College, Melbourne; Rachel Street, Montreal, etc.

Its Advantages

Personal Advantages.—These are pointed out in detail in Meditations XX., XXL, and XXIV.

Advantages to the Church and to Society.—

These are abundantly set forth in Meditations XXII. and XXIII.

Its Indulgences

The full list of the Indulgences will be found in the *Handbook of the Holy League* or in the little ID booklet *The Apostleship of Prayer* already referred to; both to be had at the *Messenger* Office, Dublin. Suffice it here to say that 159 Plenary Indulgences and a yet larger number of Partial Indulgences may be gained each year, together with participation in the prayers and good works of almost all the great religious orders and of 120 religious congregations. One hundred days' Indulgence may be gained by the Associates for every prayer or action offered for the "General Intention" of the month. These intentions are found in the monthly Calendar, and, in more extended form, in the *Messenger* itself.

Conclusion

For many reasons I have judged it best to set forth the various aspects of the Apostleship of Prayer in the form of Meditations, each divided into points. Among other advantages, this system lends itself to greater method, clearness, and precision.

XIX.—ON THE EFFICACY OF THE APOSTLESHIP OF PRAYER

1st Prelude.—Behold the Heart of Jesus in the Tabernacle as a furnace of divine love.

2nd Prelude.—Ask grace to understand what are the sources of the efficacy of the Apostleship of Prayer.

1st Point.—First source of the Efficacy of the Apostleship— Prayer.

2nd Point.—Second source—Association.

3rd Point.—Third source—Union with the Heart of Jesus.

1st Point.—First source of the Efficacy of the Apostleship— Prayer.

The vast majority of Catholics never realize the immense power they possess in prayer. It is told of the ancient philosopher Archimedes that, struck with amazement at the wonderful power of the lever, he exclaimed: "Give me a fulcrum, and I will move the world!" What in Archimedes was but a dream of the imagination, is a thing that each of us may realize in his own person. In prayer we have a lever powerful enough to move, not the material globe on which we dwell, but the Maker of all things Himself. Through prayer His omnipotence is, in a manner, placed at our disposal. God Himself, His infallible word and His promises are the fulcrum whereon we rest the irresistible lever of prayer. By prayer we help ourselves and others. By prayer we can, not only save our own immortal souls, but in addition carry on a magnificent Apostolate, by becoming instrumental in carrying out the "divinest of all works divine," the salvation and the sanctification of the souls of others. By prayer it was that the saints were what they were, and that they wrought such wonders in the cause of Christ. We have but to read the lives of a Francis Xavier, a Francis de Sales, a Vincent de Paul, to realize this fact. We, too, upon the like conditions, may seek to emulate their deeds. Need we, then, wonder at the marvelous power of the Apostleship of Prayer, as evidenced in the results it has achieved, when we consider that the instrument it uses, and from which it takes its very name, is—prayer.

2nd Point.—Second source—Association.

Of the efficacy of combined prayer we have an assurance in our Lord's own words: "Again I say to you, that if two of you shall consent upon earth, concerning anything whatsoever they shall ask, it shall be done to them by My Father who is in heaven" (Matthew xviii. 19). And immediately He explains the reason: "For where there are two or three gathered together in My name, there am I in the midst of them" (Matthew xviii. 20). What, then, shall we say of the efficacy of the supplication in which, not merely two or three, but some five and twenty million people united together to storm, as it were, the Heart of Christ with their petitions. Even in the natural order association is a source of strength. Everywhere around us we find individuals combining together for the attainment of the objects that they have in view. We see around us everywhere trades unions and associations and combinations of persons banded together for the promotion of their mutual interests. Association is no less a source of power in the supernatural than in the natural order. In nothing is its effect more efficacious than in this matter of prayer. The more numerous the hands that move the lever the more irresistible is its power.

3rd Point.—Third source—Union with the Heart of Jesus.

The sanctification of our own souls and our power under God to save and sanctify the souls of others are proportioned to the degree in which we are united with God. It is only as instruments in God's hands that we can ever hope to do His work. Furthermore, the instrument is powerless to act except in so far as it is united with the agent that makes use of it: thus, the pen cannot write unless held in the hand of the writer, nor the organ give forth music unless touched by the fingers of the musician. Now the aim and effect of the Apostleship of Prayer is to unite us with the Sacred Heart. It unites us by proposing to our zeal the same objects as those that interest and move the Heart of Christ, by seeking to make His interests ours; it unites us by increasing our devotion to the Blessed Eucharist, by drawing us more frequently to Communion, by urging us to unite our thoughts and words and actions with His, in a word, by drawing us, in our entire supernatural life, more closely to the Sacred Heart, till, with the Apostle, we can say: "I live, not I, but Christ liveth in me."

XX.- ON THE ADVANTAGES AND BENEFITS OF THE APOSTLESHIP OF PRAYER—No. 1

These advantages naturally divide themselves under four heads: (1) the *merit* it procures us; (2) the *satisfaction* it enables us to make to God for our offences; (3) the power of *impetration* it gives to obtain favors from the Sacred Heart; (4) the *strength* and *grace* it sheds upon the soul. In this meditation we shall consider the first two of these advantages.

1st Prelude.—Imagine Christ saying to you: "Child, give Me thy heart."

2nd Prelude.—Ask light and grace to understand the advantages and benefits of the Apostleship of Prayer.

1st Point.—The Apostleship of Prayer an abundant Source of Merit.

2nd Point.—The Apostleship of Prayer a means of making abundant Satisfaction for Sin.

1st Point.—The Apostleship of Prayer an Abundant Source of Merit.

1. *Merit,* in its broader acceptation, may be defined as the spiritual capital or

riches which the soul amasses in this world, wherewith to purchase its degree of everlasting happiness and glory in eternity. Nothing except mortal sin can deprive us of this merit. Tepidity and venial sin, though they retard us in acquiring it, do not diminish it when once acquired. Mortal sin alone can rob us of it, and even then, on being restored to grace, the soul gets back *in full* the degree of merit it possessed before its fall. Every supernatural act, performed with proper dispositions, in the state of grace, is meritorious, but by no means in the same degree. There are as many *grades* of merit as there are *ways* or attendant circumstances under which the self-same act may be performed. Is there, then, a secret of amassing treasure quickly; of making, so to speak, one's spiritual fortune in a short time? It must be so, for saints like Aloysius and young Stanislaus gathered more of these heavenly riches in a short few years than others in a long life. Yes, there *is* a secret, and what is more the Apostleship of Prayer affords us just the very easiest way of learning it and putting what it tells us into practice. Let us see how this is.

2. Merit arises from *two sources—(a)* the *perfection of the motive,* and *(b)* the *fervor of the will.*

As regards the *motive, three things* may influence us in our supernatural actions; the *glory of God, our own spiritual advantage,* and *the advantage of our neighbor.* Nevertheless in the supernatural order there are but *two motives,* one regarding *ourselves,* the other regarding *God;* hence there are *two kinds of charity:* the charity of *concupiscence,* which urges us to love God for our own sakes, and the charity of *benevolence,* urging us to love God for Himself. Now the motive put before us in the Apostleship of Prayer is one springing from the charity of benevolence. It teaches us to go outside ourselves, to endeavor to promote, not our own interests, but those of the Sacred Heart. Hence the motive it proposes is most perfect.

The second element that determines merit is the *fervor of the will.* Now the Apostleship of Prayer aims at objects that are eminently calculated to arouse this fervor. It makes it its endeavor in each and every action of our life to advance the interests of our Lord. It helps us to realize that every act of ours may be made conducive towards the salvation of a soul, towards obtaining the final grace of repentance for a dying sinner, or advancing God's extrinsic glory in some degree.

2nd Point.—The Apostleship of Prayer a Means of making abundant Satisfaction for Sin.

Our supernatural works are not merely a source of merit, but also a means of satisfying for our sins. This satisfactory power of our actions is augmented from three principal sources: (i) the *contrition* that accompanies them; (2) the *charity* that animates them; (3) the *benefit resulting* from them *for the neighbor.*

1. *Contrition* or *penance* is the grief experienced by the soul at the violation of God's rights, together with a corresponding impulse of the will to avenge the violation of these rights. It implies hatred of sin and desire to atone for it. Now, the exercises of the Apostleship of Prayer are a constant effort to *destroy* sin and to make *atonement* to the outraged majesty of Christ for sin. They are largely an immolation, in union with the Sacred Heart of Jesus, in atonement for the crimes of men.

2. *Charity,* as has been shown in the previous point, is perfected within us by the practices of the Apostleship of Prayer, seeing that the Apostleship is itself the most heavenly, the purest, the most energetic, the most perfect exercise of charity.

3. The Apostleship of Prayer is pre-eminently an exercise of *zeal for souls.* One of its chief aims is to draw souls from the paths of perdition to the fervent love and service of the Sacred Heart. Furthermore, exercises offered in atonement for the sins of others are an excellent atonement for our own offences. Hence it is clear that the Apostleship of Prayer is a most excellent means of making satisfaction for sin.

XXI.—ON THE ADVANTAGES AND BENEFITS OF THE APOSTLESHIP OF PRAYER—No. 2

The advantages of the Apostleship of Prayer, as was pointed out in the last Meditation, naturally divide themselves under four heads: of these we have already meditated on the first two. We now proceed to reflect on the remaining two heads of thought—namely: (3) the power of *impetration* it gives, to obtain favors from the Sacred Heart; (4) the *strength* and *peace* it sheds upon the soul.

1st Prelude.—Hear Christ saying to you: " Child, give Me thy heart?'

2nd Prelude.—Ask light and grace to understand the advantages and benefits of the Apostleship of Prayer.

3rd Point.—The Apostleship of Prayer gives great power of Impetration, to enable us to obtain favors from the Sacred Heart.

4th Point.—The Apostleship of Prayer an abundant source of Peace and Consolation.

3rd Point.—The Apostleship of Prayer gives GREAT POWER OF IMPETRATION, TO ENABLE US to obtain Favors from the Sacred Heart.

The more closely the soul is united with God, and the more it lays aside self and the interests of self, in order to belong entirely to God, and seek *His* interests alone, the greater is its power of impetrating favors for itself and others. Now the central idea of the Apostleship of Prayer is that, putting self in some degree aside, we strive in all things to promote the interests and advance the honor of the Sacred Heart. And this we do by means of *prayer*, which, of its very nature, tends to unite the soul with God. Moreover, this earnest, persevering zeal for the interests of the Sacred Heart is, itself, the highest form of the love of God, and its most practical and genuine expression. For St. Ignatius, in his Contemplation on Divine Love, assures us that love consists rather in actions than in words or mere affections of the heart.

It may, therefore, be admitted that the Apostleship of Prayer is a powerful means to unite the soul with God in the bonds of love, and enable it to put aside self in order to seek the interests of God alone, and therefore, when properly understood and practiced, it gives us great credit with Almighty God, and is a sovereign means of enabling us to obtain from Him every grace and blessing that we ask for. It leads us to forget, in a manner, our own private interests, temporal and spiritual, and in all we do, say, think, and suffer, to seek in the first place the honor and the interests of the Sacred Heart. We pray, suffer, labor, for those whom we have never known or seen, simply because their souls are inexpressibly dear to Jesus Christ, who died for them, and because we would fain bring them to glorify His name in heaven throughout eternity. Thus we make the interests of the Sacred Heart our own, we act the part of a true friend to His friend, we do what our Lord asked of St. Teresa:" Henceforth as My true spouse you will be zealous for My honor alone." From that day forth she became a saint and had immense power with God. We cannot doubt that, if we *really* practice it, the Apostleship of Prayer will do the same for us, it will become the channel of wondrous heavenly gifts and favors to our souls, and procure for us a marvelous power with Almighty God.

N.B.—*The long list of thanksgivings published month after month in the "Messenger," is, itself alone, a convincing proof of the power of the Apostleship of Prayer in obtaining favors from the Sacred Heart.*

4th Point.—The Apostleship of Prayer an Abundant Source of Peace and Consolation.

1. After God's grace, peace of heart is one of the greatest blessings in this life. It is

the first thing the angels wish to men at the birth of the Savior: *"Peace* on earth to men of good will." Christ Himself bade His disciples to invoke it, the first thing, on all to whom they preached: "Into whatsoever house ye shall enter, first say *peace* to this household." After His Resurrection the first word He addressed to them was to wish them *peace: "Pax vobis: Peace* be to you." Again and again in its liturgy the Church prays for peace for its children. Thus, in the Mass, the priest, when signing the chalice with the Host, says: "May the *peace* of the Lord be always with you," and again, at the "Agnus Dei," "Give us *peace."* Again, at Confirmation the bishop dismisses the person confirmed with the words: *"Pax tecum: Peace* be with you." Peace is therefore a great blessing; and it is, as I shall show, one of the fruits of the Apostleship of Prayer.

2. Loss of peace arises from the want of union of our wills with that of God. Conformity to God's Will is the secret of true peace of soul. Without this conformity there is a conflict between the soul and God, whereby the soul seeks its satisfaction in itself or in something that lies outside the appointed end of its existence. Now, as we have seen in the previous point, the Apostleship of Prayer leads us to put the interests of Jesus Christ before our own, it broadens our horizon and enables us to look forth across the narrow sphere of self upon the great broad ocean of God's everlasting interests out beyond us. This is the partial shutting out of self and the embracing of God's will that are the necessary condition of true peace. In this way the Apostleship of Prayer raises us to a higher, purer, nobler atmosphere. It lifts us up above the sordid aims and low degraded motives of the world into a sphere of holiness and strength and peace—the peace that flows from union with the Heart of Christ.

XXII.—ON THE ADVANTAGES RESULTING TO THE CHURCH FROM THE APOSTLESHIP OF PRAYER

One of the effects of the Apostleship of Prayer is that it takes us out of our own small selves, widens our outlook, and withdrawing us from the spiritual selfishness or individualism to which we are so prone, it enables us to realize that we are members of the great body of the Church, and have, in consequence, duties to discharge and interests to promote that lie beyond the narrow range of our own immediate personal surroundings.

1st Prelude.- -Imagine you behold two opposing standards round which are gathered two great armies, under their respective leaders, Christ and Lucifer.

2nd Prelude.—Ask grace to understand how the Apostleship of Prayer enables us to promote the cause of our great Leader, Jesus Christ.

1st *Point.*—The Apostleship of Prayer and the Communion of Saints.

2nd Point.—The Apostleship of Prayer and the Growth and Defense of the Church.

3rd Point.—The Apostleship of Prayer and Apostolic Vocations.

4th Point.—The Apostleship of Prayer unites the members of the Church.

1st Point.—The Apostleship of Prayer and the Communion of Saints.

The Church is divided into three parts: the Church *militant,* the Church *suffering,* and the Church *triumphant*; or, in other words, the Church on *earth,* in *purgatory,* and in *heaven.* The close and wonderful union that exists between these various parts is called the Communion of Saints. One of the functions of the Apostleship of Prayer is to promote this blessed union. For *first,* the binding power of this union is community of interest. The sanctification of the individual, through the advancement of God's greater glory, is the object of the Apostleship. The holier and more numerous the individuals that make up the body, the happier and holier is the general body itself. Thus, we may believe that an increase of accidental happiness occurs to the inhabitants of heaven for every accession to their number or to the individual sanctity of those to be received among them. The same, in due proportion, may be said of the Church militant. The Apostleship of Prayer tends to sanctify the Church.

Again, *prayer* is the cement that under God binds together the various portions of the Church. Prayer is the great want of the Church, the very atmosphere that sustains and invigorates its spiritual life. Whatever promotes prayer in the Church promotes the Church's life and strengthens and invigorates it. Whatever lessens or withdraws from prayer weakens the vital action of the Church. The maintenance of the spirit of prayer within the Church's bosom is, in fact, a matter of life and death with it. Now, the promotion of the spirit of prayer is, as its name implies, one of the great objects of the Apostleship of Prayer.

Catholics in the state of sanctifying grace are in common possessed, besides, of four great supernatural blessings: merit, power of offering satisfaction for sin, actual grace, and supernatural consolations. Of these, merit is incommunicable. The Communion of Saints is, therefore, confined to the last three kinds of blessings. We may help to atone for another's sin and thereby shorten his purgatory, we may secure for him actual graces, we may procure him spiritual consolation; but of these three the actual grace that may bring him to eternal happiness is undoubtedly the greatest. This is the aim of the Apostleship of Prayer. It seeks to get for frail humanity the actual graces that will win them heaven.

2nd Point.—The Apostleship of Prayer and the Growth and Defense of the Church.

In addition to sanctifying those within the Church, the Apostleship of Prayer aims at saving those who are as yet outside the household of the faith. The Church is ever seeking for the poor lost sheep that wander in the deserts of infidelity; it is ever striving to bring the saving light of the Gospel into the hearts of those that sadly sit in darkness and the shadow of death. And here it is, especially, that the Apostleship of Prayer finds scope for its consuming energies. To the weary laborers worn with fatigue who nobly strive to cultivate a barren soil, it brings the refreshing dew of prayer to water the parched earth and enable it to bring forth fruit of souls. Do not the letters of St. Francis Xavier bear abundant testimony to the amazing help he got from the prayers of his brethren and of the faithful here in Europe? Does not St. Teresa bid her children offer up their prayers and tears for the conversion of the lands that lie in darkness? This surely is the work of the Apostleship of Prayer to carry efficacious help to the brave hunters after souls in pagan lands.

And, furthermore, it arms the champions of the faith at home to fight successfully the battle with the forces of evil that are manifold and powerful around them.

3rd Point.—The Apostleship of Prayer and Apostolic Vocations.

From the preceding point it may naturally be deduced that the Apostleship of Prayer tends to foster apostolic vocations. When zeal for God's glory takes possession of young hearts, it often urges them to devote themselves to His immediate service as missionary priests and nuns. The same holy influence will urge on Catholic mothers to foster the vocations of their children. The voice of a perishing people will echo in the ears of its future missionaries, crying aloud: "Cross the seas and come to our assistance." Listen to the words of St. Francis Xavier: "How greatly do those unhappy people deceive themselves who only employ for their own advancement and honor the talents and knowledge entrusted to them by God for the good of others! How fearful the reckoning for their learning and talents! How often have I thought of returning to Europe, even if taken for a madman for so doing, and visiting every university, especially that of Paris, to proclaim to the learned men therein assembled who have more knowledge than fear of God: 'it is through your fault and negligence that numberless souls are excluded from the kingdom of heaven, and are plunged in the everlasting abyss of hell!'"

4th Point.—The Apostleship of Prayer unites the Members of the Church.

The Apostleship of Prayer offers to all the members of the Church a common interest. It invites them, from the youngest to the oldest, to concentrate their energies on one great task, to devote to it their prayers and actions, thoughts and sufferings, every faculty of soul and sense of body, and all the gifts of nature and of grace. This object is the advancement of the interests of the Sacred Heart. Assuredly, such unanimity of aim and purpose cannot but engender unity of action and bind together all the faithful into one great army of Apostles of the Sacred Heart.

XXIII.—ON THE ADVANTAGES TO SOCIETY, SECURED BY THE APOSTLESHIP OF PRAYER

In so far as the *Apostleship of Prayer* influences the individual, so far, too, does it exercise a beneficial influence upon society. The evils that afflict society arise from two main sources—*selfishness,* or the undue or unrestrained seeking after one's own personal interest, and, secondly, *forgetfulness of God* and of the duties that we owe to our Creator. To these two evil tendencies of social life the *Apostleship of Prayer* opposes (1) The Spirit of *Zeal*; and (2) the Spirit of *Prayer.*

1st Prelude.—Behold Christ saying: "I am come to cast fire upon the earth, and what will I but that it be kindled ?" (Luke xii. 49).

2nd Prelude.—Pray for the twofold spirit of zeal and of prayer.

1st Point.—Advantages resulting to the individual and to Society from the diffusion of the Spirit of Zeal.

2nd Point.—Advantages resulting to the individual and to Society from the diffusion of the Spirit of Prayer.

1st Point.—Advantages Resulting to the Individual and to Society from the Diffusion of the Spirit of Zeal.

The stability and well-being of Society rests on a triple basis: (1) Fatherly affection of superiors towards inferiors; (2) affectionate subordination of inferiors to superiors; (3) the mutual charity of members for each other. These three conditions constitute the "law of love" as applied to the three kinds of relations that exist in Society.

The practical observance of this "law of love " will induce *those in authority* to act in a kindly and considerate way to their subordinates. It will banish injustice, tyranny, oppression. It will urge *inferiors,* instead of being discontented with their lot and rising in rebellion against authority, to respect and love those over them. *Mutual Charity* and forbearance will be the blessed bond of union that ensures the inestimable blessings of harmony and peace. Strikes and revolutions and the war of classes will yield to this mutual self-sacrifice. This is exactly what is not. The clash of interests divides the parents from the children, and the children from each other. Thus, the relations of the *home* are dislocated, and happiness is lost; and in the wider sphere of *nations,* wars spread death and desolation through the earth.

It all arises from the root of selfishness. But in the *Apostleship of Prayer* we have a remedy. It will broaden and expand our outlook. As the traveler on a lofty mountain takes a broad and comprehensive view of the surrounding country, and overlooks the trifling inequalities of the expanding plain below, so, too, does the *Apostleship of Prayer* place us on a sacred pinnacle above the jarring passions of the world, its class distinctions, its feverish pursuits and aims, and enables men to rise superior to the petty passions and interests of the moment. It teaches men that all are equal in the eyes of God, mere actors on the stage of life. Who does his part the best is greatest, be he prince or peasant. Heaven is the only worthy goal of their ambition. This "spiritual broadmindedness" will make us less selfish, less self-centered, and teach us to look forth, with earnest sympathetic gaze, upon the great, vast, struggling world of souls, perishing in spiritual want around us. This is the spirit of zeal that ever seeks to promote the interests of the Sacred Heart. "*Thy Kingdom Come,* "is the watchword of the *Apostleship.*

2nd Point.—Advantages Resulting to the Individual and to Society from the Diffusion of the Spirit of Prayer.

The world is lost for want of prayer. If you wish to save it, you must make it pray. If you would make your own poor efforts fruitful, you must pray yourself. Prayer is the essential condition of salvation—the essential condition, too, of fruitful work for God. The world talks of progress. It boasts aloud of its efforts for "the amelioration of the race," and so forth. The "race" is not a whit the better for its efforts; rather less so. Poverty and crime and sorrow are as widespread now as ever.

The panaceas of the world are a failure. Prayer, and the graces it alone can win, are the only real and efficacious remedy for all the miseries of mankind. This is the remedy proposed by the *Apostleship of Prayer,* its very *raison d'etre.* Prayer has got a salve for every sorrow, a cure for all disorders. It will teach the rich and powerful to be considerate and kind to their inferiors. It will fill the poor with humble resignation to their lot. It will banish the dissensions and bridge across the chasms that divide the different classes of Society. Such is the work of the *Apostleship of Prayer*: it teaches men to pray, it thereby ennobles and elevates them, it spiritualizes their entire lives, it draws them ever nearer to the Fount of charity and grace and strength—the Sacred Heart of Jesus in the Blessed Sacrament.

XXIV.—ON THE APOSTLESHIP OF PRAYER AS A PLEDGE OF SALVATION

1st Prelude.—Imagine Jesus in the Garden of Olives beholding the vast army of sinners, who in all ages would be lost in spite of all His sufferings, and lamenting in the words of the Psalmist: " What profit is there in My Blood?" (Psalm XXIX. 10).

2nd Prelude.—Ask grace to understand how the Apostleship of Prayer endeavors to render the Precious Blood of the Redeemer fruitful in saving souls.

1st Point.—The Apostleship of Prayer a Pledge of Salvation.

2nd Point.—Sayings and Opinions of the Saints.

1st Point.—The Apostleship of Prayer a Pledge of Salvation.

The watchword of the Apostleship of Prayer is no other than *Thy Kingdom Come.* Its aim is to propagate the Kingdom of Christ by promoting the interests of the Sacred Heart. Its essential spirit is zeal for souls. In this very fact its members have a sort of guarantee of their own personal predestination. For how can we imagine that God would allow a soul to be forever lost whose great aim through life had been to enlarge His Kingdom and promote His interests? Can we imagine that God will allow to fall into hell a soul that has been directly instrumental in bringing many other souls to Him? If He promises eternal life to such as exercise the corporal works of mercy—who, in the person of His brethren, give Him to eat and to drink; who clothe and visit and console Him in the day of tribulation; how much more will He reward the far more meritorious spiritual works of mercy? Does He not hunger and thirst in the person of the sinner, whose soul is starving in the far-off land of sin, or who has withdrawn from the saving fountains of God's grace? How great, think you, will be the gratitude of the Good Shepherd to those who, by their prayers and good works, aid Him in searching for and bringing back the poor lost sheep?

Yet this is the function of the Apostleship of Prayer, to help our Savior in His work, to make His Precious Blood fruitful in the souls for which He died, to save His Life and Death and the Redemption that He wrought from being a failure.

Even we ourselves are deeply grateful to those who help us in accomplishing a work that we have very much at heart, especially if it happens to have cost us very great pain or trouble or expense. We never forget it to them. Can we then imagine that our Lord, Who is goodness and loving gratitude itself, will ever allow those to perish miserably who have assisted Him, through the Apostleship of Prayer, in saving the poor souls for which He gave His very Life in agony on Calvary? Nay, further, can we imagine that His Mother, the Refuge of Sinners and their Mother, will ever abandon those who have helped to bring back her wandering children to her side? Hence, I do not hesitate to say that zealous members of the Apostleship of Prayer have, in that very fact, a pledge and guarantee of everlasting life.

2nd Point.—Sayings and Opinions of the Saints.

The lives of the saints abound in testimonies to the truth of what has just been said. Their greatest characteristic was their burning zeal for souls. St. Paul wished even to be "anathema from Christ" for the salvation of his brethren (Romans ix. 3). St. Ignatius would risk his own salvation to bring souls to God. St. Francis de Sales would give up all else if only he could save poor erring souls from hell. And the very vehemence—shall I call it extravagance? —of their zeal made those men the saints they were. God rewarded their forgetfulness of self in His behalf by granting them the very highest gifts of grace. St. Catherine of Siena tells us: "There is not on earth a more consoling or more useful work" than thus to devote oneself to the extension of God's Kingdom in this world. "I burn," she adds, "to give my blood, my life, the marrow of my bones for holy Church, sinner as I am."

Our Lord once appeared to St. Gertrude bearing on His shoulders a magnificent building. This He told her was the Church, which He said was "tending to ruin throughout the world, because there are so few who are willing to do or suffer anything for its support. ... You must . . . afford Me relief by sharing with Me the weight of this load." St. Mary Magdalen of Pazzi, fifty times a day, offered the Precious Blood of Christ to God for sinners, and in ecstasy of zeal for their conversion cried aloud : " How great is the trouble that I feel, O my God ! when I see I might be of use to Thy creatures by giving my life for theirs, and I have not the liberty of doing so!" Another saintly soul would cry: "I find no repose, O my God, so long as there is a corner of the earth in which Thou art neither known nor loved." St. Liguori says: "All those who truly love God pray unceasingly for sinners" (St. Liguori on Prayer). Thus, extracts might be multiplied to show that sanctity and zeal for souls are interchangeable and correlative, and that God rewards our zeal for His interests by bringing us to everlasting life.

XXV.—ON THE "THREE DEGREES" OF THE APOSTLESHIP OF PRAYER

1st Prelude.—Behold Jesus in the tabernacle ever offering up a prayer of priceless value to His Heavenly Father for the salvation of souls and for the welfare of His Church.

2nd Prelude.—Ask grace to realize the meaning and importance of the "*Three Degrees*" of the Apostleship of Prayer.

1st *Point.*—Meaning and Importance of the "First Degree."

2nd *Point.*—Meaning and Importance of the "Second Degree."

3rd *Point.* — Meaning and Importance of the "Third Degree."

1st Point.—Meaning and Importance of the "First Degree."

The life of Jesus in the tabernacle is a life of constant prayer and union with His Heavenly Father. As Redeemer of the human race, His powerful pleadings rise like sweetest incense to the throne of God, to draw down countless blessings on His creatures. His presence in the Blessed Eucharist is an endless renewal of His immolation on the hill of Calvary. By it He carries on incessantly the work of saving souls. In this great undertaking He, so to speak, looks round for instruments to aid Him, who will join Him, and be, as it were, His *fellow workers* and *Apostles* in the glorious task of winning souls to God. From within the narrow limits of the tabernacle He guides and governs and helps the Church. He invites us—wondrous privilege!—to assist Him by our *prayers.* He would have us pray and work and suffer *in union with Him* and *for His intentions.* Our daily actions, even to the smallest offered in the state of grace *to* God, and done *for* God, are equivalent to so much prayer, and share the characteristics of a sacrificial act, in that their power is impetratory, sacrificial, eucharistic. The "First Degree," consisting in the *"Morning Offering"* of the thoughts, words, actions, sufferings of the day, ennobles all we do, spiritualizes our entire life, by offering up to Jesus through Mary's hands our every act, for the intentions of His Sacred Heart. Moreover, this is done by each, not merely by himself alone, but as a member of a vast and world-wide organization, embracing, like a mighty army, in its ranks some five-and-twenty millions of the faithful fervent soldiers, worshippers, and clients of the Sacred Heart. Thus, the members of this wonderful association are *Apostles. Prayer* is their great weapon. Hence its title *The Apostleship of Prayer.* Hence, too, its cry of battle is *"Thy Kingdom Come."*

2nd Point.—Meaning and Importance of the "Second Degree."

In the great campaign on which we have entered, to further and defend the interests of the Sacred Heart, we naturally invoke the aid of Mary. The Mother is necessarily the champion of the Son. She is our natural ally. She is our advocate, "powerful as an army in battle array." She is our Queen and Leader, under whose banner, which is also that of her Divine Son, we are sure to be victorious in our struggle with the hosts of Satan. We therefore call on her to help us by the *"Daily Decade"* offered for the Pope's intention. The Pope, as Vicar and Vicegerent of our Lord on earth, assigns each month a special intention to be prayed for. This intention, thus chosen by the Sovereign Pontiff, is one that most intimately concerns the welfare of the Church. It is an intention that is vital to the interests of the Sacred Heart. On it are concentrated for the month the efforts of this powerful and world-wide association of the *Apostleship of Prayer* with all its vast machinery of prayer and impetration. At the word of command from the Pope the *Daily Decade,* like a battering ram, backed up and strengthened by the *Morning Offering,* is directed against a given portion of the enemy's fortress, till it reels and falls beneath repeated blows. Next month another portion is selected for attack, and thus the foe is driven back at every point. Even apart from the special power of united prayer, the *Daily Decade* imports into one's life a large amount of prayer each day and helps to raise us higher in the ranks of the great army of soldiers and apostles of the Sacred Heart.

3rd Point.—Meaning and Importance of the "Third Degree."

"I looked for one that would grieve together with me, but there was none: and for one that would comfort me, and I found none " (Psalm lxviii. 21), are the plaintive words in which, by the lips of the Psalmist, the Redeemer grieves over the ingratitude of men. "Men," He once said to Blessed Margaret Mary, "show Me nothing but coldness and indifference, but do thou at least give Me pleasure by making atonement for their ingratitude." And the "atonement" that He asked of her was the reception of the Blessed Eucharist "as an act of thanksgiving and reparation every First Friday." Besides giving our Blessed Lord this "pleasure" by going to Communion on the First Friday, the *Third Degree* aims at offering to the Sacred Heart a vast number of *daily* communions *made in turn* by the associates as a *perpetual* offering of reparation. This constant and assiduous oblation must be very pleasing to our Lord and must render those who join in it very dear to His Divine Heart.

Resolution.—To practice the Three Degrees of the Apostleship and get others to practice them.

Aspiration.—"Thy Kingdom Come."

XXVI.—ON THE "MORNING OFFERING" OF THE APOSTLESHIP OF PRAYER

1st Prelude.—Imagine Mary offering your prayers, works, and sufferings to the Sacred Heart.

2nd Prelude.—Ask grace to understand the value and importance of the "Morning Offering."

1st *Point.*— "O Jesus, through the most pure heart of Mary." To Whom and through Whom do we make the "Morning Offering"?

2nd Point.—"I offer Thee all the prayers, works, and sufferings of this day." What is it that we offer?

3rd Point.—"For all the Intentions of Thy Divine Heart." For what object and intention do we make our Offering?

1st Point.—"O Jesus, through the Most Pure Heart of Mary." To Whom and through Whom do we make the "MORNING Offering"?

To Whom? To *Jesus Christ* the Second Person of the Blessed Trinity made Man, who as God is our *Creator,* and entitled by virtue of creation and conservation to the possession of our entire being, body and soul; Who as Man is our *Redeemer* and has purchased us at the price of His precious Blood— rescued us, at infinite cost to Himself, from hell and from the devil, and is therefore entitled to our everlasting gratitude and love and service; Who, moreover, is our great *King* and *Leader,* and Whom we should, therefore, follow and fight for as brave soldiers; Who is our best and truest *Friend,* and as such entitled to our confidence and love; the *Physician* of our souls to Whom we ought to turn for succor in our spiritual maladies; Who, in fine, has made such wondrous promises to those who are devoted to His Sacred Heart.

Through Whom? Through the *Most Pure Heart of* our own dear Mother *Mary.* Penetrated with the thought of our unworthiness, we shrink, perhaps, from approaching God directly. We, therefore, take Mary as mediatrix between us and her Divine Son. For *her* sake He will look with favor on our poor, unworthy prayers. Passing through *her* hands, our poor, unworthy gifts, the offerings that we make, will acquire a value and importance quite beyond their own intrinsic worth. *All for Jesus through Mary* must be our motto; her Heart is an alembic that changes all that passes through it into purest gold.

2nd Point.—"I offer Thee all the Prayers, Works, and Sufferings of this Day." What is it that we OFFER?

1. *Our Prayers.* How cold, how negligently said, how distracted they are! How little fervor there is in them I Yet passing through the heart of Mary in they reach the Heart of Jesus purified, inflamed, and glowing with the love of God, as iron, itself so hard and cold, is kindled into glowing heat and softened in its passage through the furnace.

2. *Our Works.* We work perhaps hard throughout the day, our lives are lives of labor; yet, mayhap, for lack of pure intention we lose much, if not all, of the precious fruits that might be gained of merit here and of reward in heaven. 'Twere sad tot oil through life yet reach the gates of death with empty hands. To do so were laboriously to gather treasures in a sieve that lets them fall to earth ere yet they have been grasped. But offered up each day through Mary's hands, the labors and duties of the day, the material occupations that take up so large a portion of our lives, have each their corresponding merit and reward in heaven,

and will be found, hereafter, written in the Book of Life in characters of gold.

3. *Our Sufferings.* The sufferings and the sorrows of this life may easily be rendered our most valuable assets for eternity. Their atoning power is immense. In God's intention they are meant to sanctify and cleanse the soul from sin and its results. They are the meritorious though mitigated purgatory of the elect. Yet not only may we forfeit all their value by not bearing them with proper dispositions, but by murmur or revolt against the will of God, we may make them means of adding fuel to the purgatorial fires that await us. To sanctify our sufferings is a matter of supreme importance for us. In no way can we better do so than by offering them to Jesus through the Heart of Mary, and in union with the sorrows of these two most suffering and afflicted of all human hearts.

3rd Point.—"For all the Intentions of thy Divine Heart." For what Object and Intention do we make our Offering?

What intentions could there possibly be, nobler, more urgent, or more pleasing to Almighty God than those of the Sacred Heart of Jesus Christ Himself? What prayer more pleasing to our Blessed Lord than that which is offered for His own intentions? We feel grateful to those that join with us in praying for intentions we have very much at heart. We can give no better testimony of our affection or good-will towards anyone than by praying for his intentions. And so, by praying for the intentions of the Heart of Jesus, we are offering Him the best and most acceptable testimony of our love. As faithful, loyal soldiers of the Sacred Heart we are doing battle for His interests. And when the field is fought and won, and the day of everlasting triumph is at hand, may not the clients of the Sacred Heart who have been faithful to the "Morning Offering," day by day, expect to hear from the lips of their King and Captain, Jesus Christ, the thrilling words of praise: "Well done, good and faithful servant . . . enter thou into the joy of thy Lord (Matthew XXV. 23).

Resolution.—To be faithful to the "Morning Offering."

Ejaculation.—Thy Kingdom Come!

XXVII.—ON THE GENERAL PRACTICE OF THE APOSTLESHIP OF PRAYER

1st Prelude.—Behold Christ saying to the seventy-two disciples: "The harvest indeed is great but the laborers are few. Pray ye therefore the Lord of the harvest that He send laborers into His harvest" (Luke x. 2).

2nd Prelude.—Ask grace to understand and put in practice the exercises of the Apostleship of Prayer.

The full official title of the Apostleship is, *"The Apostleship of Prayer: a Holy League of Christian Hearts united with the Heart of Jesus to obtain the Triumph of the Church and of the Holy See and the Salvation of Souls"* It is, therefore, (1) an *"Apostleship"—i.e.,* an association consisting of persons who constitute themselves "Apostles" to promote the interests of the Sacred Heart. (2) An Apostleship of "Prayer"—*i.e.,* prayer is the great *means* it adopts to attain its objects. (3) A "League *of Christian Hearts:"* hence a *united and organized body* banded together for the attaining of a common object. (4) "United *with the Heart of Jesus"*: hence Jesus Christ is the Captain and Leader of this League; it looks for the success of its endeavors to His Sacred Heart, and seeks in close union with that Divine Heart to secure the abundant graces necessary for success. (5) Its object is two-fold: *(a) the Triumph of the Church and of the Holy See;* and (b) *the Salvation of Souls.* Its organ is the *Messenger of the Sacred Heart.* There are, in all, forty-two *Messengers* published in twenty-seven languages. It numbers about 25,000,000 associates, scattered over the whole of the civilized world. It shares in the merits and good works of practically all the Religious Orders in the Church. In various ways, and especially through what is termed the "Treasury of Good Works," each member shares in the prayers and good works of all the rest. It is, in short, a vast and world-wide organization of prayer to promote the interests of the Sacred Heart, the salvation of souls, and the salvation and sanctification of its individual members.

We do not propose to do more than merely *suggest* practices of devotion to the Sacred Heart. Spiritual tastes and attractions differ widely, and each one will best be able to choose what suits himself. It is also well to distinguish between what is essential and what is not essential. "Four things," says Father Nolden, S.J., in his excellent book on *Devotion to the Sacred Heart,* "are essential to this devotion: *adoration,* because it is a divine heart; *imitation,* because it is the holiest of hearts; a *return of love,* because it is the most loving of hearts; and *reparation,* because it is the least known, the least appreciated of hearts."

The practices of the Apostleship of Prayer may be divided into three principal classes: (1) Those that directly regard *God;* (2) those that directly regard *ourselves;* (3) those that directly regard our *neighbor.*

1st Point.—Practices regarding God.

2nd Point.—Practices regarding Ourselves.

3rd Point.—Practices regarding our Neighbor.

1st Point.—Practices regarding God.

These are mainly adoration and reparation. Foremost among the ways of discharging these two duties are *Mass* and *Holy Communion.* In a single Mass we may offer more glory and reparation to the Sacred Heart than by all our other exercises put together. Again, by the fervor of our Communions we offer immense homage and reparation to our Lord. Hence the monthly and weekly Communions of reparation peculiar to the Third Degree hold the highest place among the practices of this devotion. There is no better form of devotion to the Sacred Heart than the practice, so earnestly recommended by the Holy See, of daily Mass and daily Communion offered in Its honor. (2) *Meditation* comes next in importance. There are plenty of books of meditation on the Sacred Heart to be had nowadays. Moreover, other meditations, especially those on the Life and Passion of our Lord, may easily be turned in on devotion to the Sacred Heart. Meditation teaches us how to *imitate* the Sacred Heart. (3) *Reading* goes hand in hand with meditation. The monthly *Messenger of the Sacred Heart* affords excellent spiritual reading and usually contains a special meditation on the Sacred Heart. (4) Devotion to the *Blessed Sacrament,* especially that which takes the form of visits of reparation, or the exercises of the Guard of Honor, of the Association of Perpetual Adoration, or of the Holy Hour, is also to be highly recommended. (5) Next comes the *Daily Decade* for the Pope's intention which constitutes the Second Degree. (6) Various *subsidiary devotions—e.g.,* to the Passion, to the Immaculate Heart of Mary, to St. Joseph, to the Holy Angels, to the Souls in Purgatory, may all be pressed into the service and be made so many means of increasing our devotion to the Sacred Heart.

2nd Point.—Practices regarding Ourselves.

First among these comes the *consecration of ourselves to the Sacred Heart.* This is a point of very great importance. It enables us to fulfil our fourth essential duty, that of making a return of love for love. Every client of the Sacred Heart should make an entire and unreserved oblation of himself and all that he has and is—his body with its senses, his soul with all its faculties and powers, every thought, word, action, and suffering of his life; in a word, his entire being, to become, both in time and in eternity, the absolute property and possession of the Sacred Heart. This oblation should often be renewed, especially on each First Friday of the month. Thus, one's whole being becomes consecrated to the Sacred Heart. One thus lives, in a sense, in and by and for the Sacred Heart, and thus realizes the ideal of St. Paul that in Him we ought to "live and move and have our being. "Such an entire consecration of ourselves has an extraordinarily sanctifying effect upon the soul and establishes a wonderfully close bond of union between us and the Heart of Christ. (2) Closely allied with this is the practice of the *Morning Offering,* which constitutes the First Degree of the Apostleship of Prayer. By virtue of this "Offering" our every thought, word, action, or suffering becomes a new expression of our love, a fresh source of merit, another link to unite us to our Lord, a powerful help to the Church, a means of saving souls; in short, a new lever to advance the interests of the Sacred Heart.

3RD Point.—Practices regarding our Neighbor.

Zeal for souls is, as we have shown, the very essence of the Apostleship of Prayer, its very *raison d'etre.* We cannot show this zeal better than by *teaching men to know and love the Sacred Heart,* the knowledge and love of which has power to save. (2) Prayer, and especially the offering of the Holy Sacrifice, for the conversion of *sinners in their last agony* is a splendid exercise of devotion to the Sacred Heart. (3) Devotion to the *souls in purgatory* is no less dear to that compassionate and tender Heart. (4) Zeal for the *Foreign Missions,* where souls are perishing in millions for want of missionary priests and nuns to help them, gratifies one of the keenest longings of the Heart of Christ. (5) The further *Sanctification of the Just* is perhaps the most deeply seated of all the ardent desires of the Sacred Heart. By getting others to join the Apostleship of Prayer, and thus to become themselves Apostles of the Sacred Heart, you may do much to satisfy this longing of the Heart of Christ.

THE HOLY HOUR

INTRODUCTORY NOTE

The "Holy Hour" in common with other devotions connected with the Sacred Heart, is becoming wonderfully popular nowadays. In many places it forms, with the Monthly Communion of Reparation and the Exposition of the Blessed Sacrament, an integral part of the First Friday devotions, and wherever it has thus been introduced thronged churches and a wonderful increase of devotion in the faithful have been the immediate and assured result.

In convents and other religious communities, especially where the custom already exists of having "Exposition," the practice of the "Holy Hour" naturally takes a foremost place among the devotions of the First Friday.

In public churches in cities and large towns, the practice of making the Holy Hour in common on the First Friday of each month in presence of the Blessed Sacrament exposed is rapidly gaining ground, and the results that follow from this beautiful custom are in the highest degree consoling.

The method of thus making it is set forth in the section entitled, "Practice *of the Holy Hour in Common*" given below. Generally speaking, from two o'clock to three o'clock, or in the evening about half-past seven, will be found the most convenient hour.

As Will be seen from the following pages, the devotion of the "Holy Hour " has received not merely the sanction but also the warm approval of the Holy See, in the persons of Pius VIII., Gregory XVI., Pius IX., and most of all of Leo XIII. It is, therefore, a safe and solid exercise of devotion to the Sacred Heart.

N.B.—As will be seen in the article in the following pages, entitled *The Statutes of the Apostleship of Prayer and the Holy Hour, all members of the Apostleship of Prayer are, by that very fact, entitled to all the privileges of the confraternity of the Holy Hour.*

I. THE HOLY HOUR

The Holy Hour is a practice of devotion taught by our Lord Himself to Blessed Margaret Mary Alacoque. The first revelation of this devotion took place on the Feast of All Saints, in the year 1673.

"On this occasion Jesus Christ," says Blessed Margaret Mary, "bid me rise every Thursday night at the hour He would appoint, in order to recite five 'Our Fathers' and five 'Hail Marys' prostrate on the earth, together with five acts of adoration which He had taught me, thus to render homage to Him in the extreme agony He suffered on the night of His Passion."

The next communication which the Saint received was in the following year, 1674. Her Divine Master appeared to her, "His wounds," she says, "shining like five suns," and rays issuing from every portion of His Sacred Humanity, especially from His Heart, which "resembled a furnace." He complained to her of the indifference with which men received the advances of His love and asked her to make atonement for their base ingratitude.

"And when I showed Him how powerless I was to do so, He replied, 'Behold, here is how I will make up for all that is wanting on your part. ... You shall receive Holy Communion on the First Friday of each month, and every night between Thursday and Friday I will make you partaker of that sorrow unto death which it was My Will to suffer in the Garden of Olives. This sorrow will reduce you, without your understanding how, to a kind of agony more bitter than death. To join with Me in the humble prayer which I then offered to My Divine Father in agony you shall rise before midnight, and remain with Me upon your knees, prostrate for an hour, with your face to the ground, to appease the anger of My Father Eternal, and to ask of Him pardon for sinners.

"You shall thus also share with Me, and in a manner soothe, the bitter grief I suffered when My disciples abandoned Me and I was constrained to reproach them that they could not watch with Me one hour. During that hour you shall do what I will teach you."

In these words of our Divine Lord we find clearly set forth the object and intention of the Holy Hour. Christ wishes His faithful friends to become, in a manner, "partakers of that sorrow unto death which it was His Will to suffer in the Garden of Olives," "to join with Him in the humble prayer which He then offered to His Father," thereby "to appease the anger" of that Heavenly Father and to ask "of Him pardon for sinners." We shall thus "share with Him, and in a manner soothe, the bitter grief He suffered when His disciples abandoned Him."

What nobler or more sublime office than to keep our Divine Lord company in His bitter agony, to take the place of His unfaithful disciples, and to console and comfort His afflicted Heart.

II. BLESSED MARGARET MARY PRACTISES THE HOLY HOUR

Here is how Blessed Margaret Mary describes the effect which the above communication had upon her. "All this time," she writes, "I was as one beside herself and unconscious of all else. When they came to bring me away, seeing that I could not speak nor even walk, except with great difficulty, they at length took me to the Rev. Mother." The poor victim of Divine Love, almost in ecstasy and trembling violently from head to foot, threw herself at the feet of her Superior, who took occasion to mortify and humble her to the utmost of her power, and ended by refusing her permission to do what her Divine Master had demanded of her. But our Lord soon wrought a change in the Superior's will.

Margaret Mary became very ill, and the doctors found themselves altogether unable to cope with her disease. At last the Superior ordered her to ask the restoration of her health from Christ, adding that if her health were restored it would be taken as a proof that her communications were from God, and she would be allowed to put in practice her desires re¬garding the First Friday Communion and the Holy Hour.

"Having represented this to our Lord by order of obedience," she says, "I was immediately restored to health."

One would think that after this test Margaret Mary might well have been allowed the free indul¬gence of the practices of devotion demanded of her by our Lord, yet from the following letter addressed in 1690 by her former Superior, Mother Greyfie, to her successor, Mother de Levy-Chateaumorand, we learn such was not the case. The letter throws an interesting light on Margaret Mary's practice of the Holy Hour.

"I do not know," wrote Mother Greyfie, in refer¬ence to Sister Margaret Mary, "whether you are aware that she was in the habit of spending an hour in prayer every night between Thursday and Friday. She began immediately after Matins and remained till eleven o'clock prostrate with face to the earth. During the time that she was suffering most I made her exchange this position for a kneeling posture, with her hands joined on her bosom. I even wished to stop her from performing this devotion altogether. She obeyed my order to this effect, but several times during this period of interruption she came to me in great anxiety and told me that she was afraid our Lord would be angry with me for what I had done, and that He would exact satisfaction from me in a way which would be very painful to me. I still refused to withdraw the prohibition, but the death of our Sister Carre and certain circumstances that accompanied the loss of this valuable subject soon forced me to change my mind and to restore her hour's prayer to Sister Margaret Mary; in fact, I could not rid myself of the conviction that this was the punishment with which she had threatened me on the part of our Divine Lord."

The Superior had learned from sad experience that it was dangerous to trifle with the orders which Margaret Mary received from her Divine Master, and so from this time forward she seems to have been left quite free to practice the Holy Hour. And not merely did she practice it herself, but there are good grounds for the belief that she strove with all the fervent energy of the love that consumed her to promote its practice, also, in her own community, and among all those with whom she came in contact.

III. FURTHER HISTORY OF THE HOLY HOUR

How different are God's ways from those of men. He is so great and powerful and far-seeing that He can afford to wait and work out His designs slowly and by degrees. And He sometimes allows whole centuries to pass without any apparent progress towards the end He has in view. So it was with regard to the devotion of the Holy Hour. God allowed a lengthened period to elapse during which this devotion lay dormant, or at most concealed within the hearts of some few chosen souls. Yet it was but gathering strength to come forth vested in a splendor and attractiveness that at once secured for it a foremost place among the practices of devotion to the Sacred Heart.

The Confraternity of the Holy Hour.

It was a brother-religious of Father de la Colombiere, the first great apostle, after Blessed Margaret Mary herself, of devotion to the Sacred Heart, who was destined in God's Providence to be instrumental in making known to the world the devotion of the Holy Hour. In 1828 the Fathers of the Society of Jesus came back once more to their ancient home in Paray-le-Monial, from which they had been driven by the Revolution. The superior of the residence was Father Debrosse, a man of remarkable virtue and holiness. The following year, 1829, he felt within himself a strong attraction urging him to make the Holy Hour in the very spot where, well-nigh a century and a half before, it had been made for the first time by Blessed Margaret Mary Alacoque herself. Hitherto he had been in the habit of making it once a year on the night of Holy Thursday; he now began to make it on the eve of each First Friday. And as he knelt one night in May, keeping his hour of loving vigil before the silent tabernacle, a voice within him spoke through the silence of his lonely watch, and bade him go forth and spread abroad the devotion of the Holy Hour. Was it a voice from heaven, or the prompting of his own deep fervent piety? He knew not; but from that day forth he strove with all his might to bring about the establishment of a Confraternity of the Holy Hour.

The project received the warm approval of the Bishop of Autun, Mgr. du Trousset d'Hericourt. Strengthened and encouraged by the support of this Prelate, Father Debrosse sent a petition to Pope Pius VIII., begging for the establishment of a Confraternity of the Holy Hour.

We may well imagine the joy of the holy priest when the Pope replied by a Brief, dated December 29, 1829, granting his request in full, and giving, moreover, a Plenary Indulgence to the members of the Confraternity every time they made the Holy Hour.

As yet the devotion was in its earliest infancy. But once fairly started it advanced with wonderful rapidity. The very next year there came a second Brief from Pius VIII., dated May 29, 1830, extending the indulgence of the Confraternity to all the faithful of the Diocese of Autun; and again a third Brief, issued by Pope Gregory XVI., July 27, 1831, made the Confraternity and its privileges world-wide. Thus three successive years mark three great stages in its progress: it was first parochial, then diocesan, lastly Catholic and universal.

Nor did its onward course stop here. By a Rescript of October 19, 1866, Pope Pius IX. allowed religious communities to be registered collectively instead of individually as had been hitherto the practice. On May 13, 1875, the same illustrious Pontiff decreed that *those who were Associates of the League of the Sacred Heart were, by that fact, entitled to gain the indulgence of the Holy Hour.*

Pope Leo XIII. and the Holy Hour.

It was reserved for the late glorious Pontiff Leo XIII. to crown and perfect the organized practice of the Holy Hour. Up to this it had been a necessary condition for the gaining of the indulgence that the Holy Hour should be made some time between Thursday evening and sunrise on Friday. In the following *Apostolic Letter,* which, on account of its importance, we quote in full, the Pope removed this restriction, and left it free to the devotion of the faithful to make the Holy Hour "on any day and at any hour during the week." Thus, the Holy Hour may now be made, and the Plenary Indulgence gained, on Friday or Sunday or any other day, and at any hour of the day that is found convenient.

For a Perpetual Remembrance.

"As the Associates of the Pious League, which is called the *Apostleship of Prayer,* and which, by the Divine favor, has spread from the Diocese of Toulouse through the whole world, are to celebrate during this year an anniversary feast, our beloved son, Julian Florian Desprez, Cardinal-Priest of the Holy Roman Church, and, by Apostolic dispensation, Archbishop of Toulouse, has earnestly entreated us that, for the spiritual good and advantage of the Associates of the said Apostleship, we should take this most favorable opportunity of granting certain favors and privileges.

"In order that so fruitful a League may receive daily greater increase, and that the Associates admitted to the League may be given further incitement to deserve well of the Catholic cause, we have resolved with a willing heart to correspond with these desires so far as we can in the Lord. And for this reason, trusting in the mercy of the Almighty God and in the authority of His Apostles, the Blessed Peter and Paul, we concede and grant the following favors:

"It has been reported to us that many Associates of the said Apostleship, duly called together by the Directors according to the Statutes of the League, are wont to assemble on certain hours and days in churches or chapels to perform, in honor of the Most Sacred Heart of Jesus or of the August Sacrament of the Altar, the pious exercises of adoration and reparation belonging to the devotion of the *Holy Hour.*

"Already, by Apostolic Letter, dated May 13, 1875, a Plenary Indulgence, to be gained once a week, had been granted to those Associates who should practice the *Holy Hour* sometime between two o'clock on Thursday and sunrise of Friday. But many of the Associates, especially working-men and domestics, would be hindered from making use and reaping the fruits of so holy an exercise if we did not confer on the said Directors the faculty of appointing a suitable day and hour.

"Therefore, that the Associates may not be restricted to so limited a time and thus be deprived of so signal a spiritual grace, we, by our Apostolical Authority and the force of these presents, grant to the Associates of the said League the faculty of performing the above-mentioned exercise of the Holy Hour *on any day, and at any hour during the week* when the local Directors shall assemble them in a church or chapel. This, however, is on condition that they shall gain the Indulgence once only each week, and that they rightly perform in the Lord the other works of piety which are enjoined them.

"Given at Rome at Saint Peter's, under the Fisherman's ring, on the 30th day of March, 1886, in the ninth year of Our Pontificate."

"M. Cardinal Ledochowski."

The Statutes of the Apostleship of Prayer and the Holy Hour.

Lastly, in the revised Statutes of the Apostleship of Prayer published by the Congregation of Bishops and Regulars at the request of the late Holy Father Leo XIII., under date July 11, 1896, Statute No. 5 is devoted to the Holy Hour and reads as follows:

"Likewise, although the pious Confraternity of the 'Holy Hour' is distinct from 'The Pious Association of the Apostleship of Prayer,' nevertheless all the Associates of the Apostleship of Prayer who duly practice this devout exercise of the 'Holy Hour' in view of appeasing the Most Sacred Heart, provoked by the outrages of mankind, and of winning a favorable hearing for our prayers, are entitled to all the spiritual graces which the Rescript of Pius IX., dated May 13, 1875, and the Brief of Leo XIII., dated March 30, 1886, grant to those who practice this pious exercise."

From this Statute we see that *to gain all the privileges attached to the Confraternity of the Holy Hour it suffices to be a Member of the Apostleship of Prayer.*

IV. NATURE OF THE HOLY HOUR

We can best understand the nature of the Holy Hour by considering the words in which our Lord Himself explained it to His servant Blessed Margaret Mary: "Every night between Thursday and Friday," He said to her, "I will make you partaker of that sorrow unto death which it was My will to suffer in the Garden of Olives. This sorrow will reduce you, without your understanding how, to a kind of agony more bitter than death. To join with Me in the humble prayer which I then offered to My Divine Father in agony, you shall rise before midnight and remain with Me upon your knees, prostrate for an hour with your face to the ground. . . . You shall thus share with Me, and in a manner soothe, the bitter grief I suffered when My disciples abandoned Me."

Hence the Holy Hour is an exercise of devotion suggested by our Lord Himself, and sanctioned and approved of by the Church, whereby we (1) become partakers of the sorrow unto death which Christ suffered in the Garden of Olives; (2) join with Him in the humble prayer which He then poured forth to His Eternal Father; (3) share with Him and soothe the bitter grief He suffered when His Disciples abandoned Him.

What nobler or more sublime exercise of devotion could there be than this, whereby we become partakers of the sorrows of the Man God, are privileged to join with Him in His prayer in the Garden, and have the supreme happiness of consoling Him in the grief He suffered at the abandonment of His disciples?

The primary idea, therefore, embodied in the Holy Hour is that of keeping our Divine Lord company in His Prayer and Agony in the Garden of Olives. All true and faithful lovers of the Sacred Heart should take as addressed to themselves those words of Christ to His Apostles when He found them sleeping: *"Could you not watch one hour with Me?"*

V. END AND OBJECT OF THE HOLY HOUR

From what has just been said it is easy to understand, at least in part, what is the end and object of the Holy Hour. However, in addition to the three ends pointed out above, there are two others which are put forward in a more formal manner by our Lord in His revelation concerning the devotion of the Holy Hour to Blessed Margaret Mary, and which were the two great objects of His own Prayer in the Garden of Olives.

"You will remain with Me upon your knees prostrate for an hour," He said to Blessed Margaret Mary, "*to appease the anger of My Eternal Father, and to ask of Him pardon for sinners*"

Here are two great ends which our Lord would have us keep in view in making the Holy Hour: the appeasing of God's anger and securing pardon and the grace of repentance for sinners. Let us consider these two ends for a moment.

The Appeasing of God's Anger.

(1) What is it that provokes God's anger?

(2) What is it that appeases it?

1. It is *sin* and sin alone that *provokes God's anger*. Sin is God's great enemy. When we sin we take up arms against God, and join with the demons, His bitterest foes, in the rebel cry, *"Non serviam—I will not serve,"* we set aside the end for which God made us, we refuse to do His bidding, and as far as the creature is capable of doing so, we strike at the very life of God Himself.

2. Hence to *appease the wrath of God* we must— (1) Avoid and detest sin in ourselves; (2) prevent it as far as we can in others; (3) make reparation for it as far as it exists in ourselves and in others. How can we do these three things? *(a)* By exciting ourselves to fervent acts of contrition, and making earnest resolutions for the future; *(b)* by praying for and helping others on towards God, and through the means of exhortation and good example influencing them for good; *(c)* lastly, by making acts of reparation.

There is a fourfold malice in sin: it is a practical denial (1) of God's sovereignty; (2) of His Goodness; (3) of His Attributes and even of His very existence; (4) it is the worship of self in preference to the worship of the Creator.

Therefore we make reparation for sin—(1) By the acknowledgment of God's sovereignty, and of His supreme dominion over us, and, consequently, by being entirely obedient and submissive to His Will, saying: Lord, I am the work of Thy hands, do with me as Thou pleasest. (2) By the acknowledgment of His goodness, and by fulfilling our corresponding duty of loving and thanking Him with our whole hearts. O Lord! Thou art love and goodness itself. I love Thee, O Jesus, with all my heart. (3) By the acknowledgment of His other attributes especially His Mercy, Justice, Omnipotence, and plenitude of all perfection. (4) By the exercise of self-denial and mortification, or self-immolation, whereby atonement in kind is made to God for seeking the satisfaction of self in preference to that of the Creator.

Asking Pardon for Sinners.

During a Retreat which Blessed Margaret Mary made in the year 1673, Christ revealed to her the manner in which He wished her to ask pardon for sinners: "You shall lift up your heart and hands," He said, "to heaven, with the offering of prayers and good works, presenting Me continually to My Father as a Victim of love, in sacrifice and oblation for the sins of the whole world, and placing Me as a secure bulwark between His justice and sinners, to obtain mercy, with which you shall feel encompassed, when I shall be pleased to grant My favors to any of these sinners. You must, then, offer Me to My Father in thanksgiving for the mercy I have shown."

Here, then, we learn from the lips of Christ how we may best obtain pardon for sinners. It is by offering our Divine Lord Himself, His Adorable Body and Blood, Soul and Divinity, in the Mass and in the Blessed Eucharist; offering, too, to His Eternal Father His life of labor ; His bitter passion and death, and every thought and action and suffering of His mortal life on earth; His five most precious wounds; the merits He amassed, and the infinite satisfaction that He made to His Eternal Father. In all this we have an infinite treasure from which we can draw at will to make atonement for our own sins and for those of all mankind.

VI. THE PRACTICE OF THE HOLY HOUR

In the second part of this book will be found various methods of making the Holy Hour. No special form of prayer or meditation is required, "but the words of our Lord to Blessed Margaret Mary seem to imply the fitness of meditating on His bitter *agony,* on His great *humiliation,* on His *love* repaid with so much ingratitude, and on the *outrages* offered to His Divine Majesty at all times, but especially during the present 'hour' " *(Irish Handbook of the Apostleship of Prayer,* p. 45, published at the office of the *Irish Messenger of the Sacred Heart,* 5, Great Denmark Street, Dublin).

The Practice in Common.

By virtue of the Brief of Pope Leo XIII., and Statute No. 5 of the revised Statutes of the Apostleship of Prayer, Diocesan or Local Directors have the power to appoint any day and hour that is found convenient for the making of the Holy Hour in common.

In Parishes and Apostleship Centers, and especially in Convents and Convent Schools, where there are weekly exercises of devotion in honor of the Sacred Heart, the time devoted to these exercises will naturally be found the most convenient for the making of the Holy Hour.

In many Churches and Convents and College Chapels throughout the country the Blessed Sacrament is exposed during at least portion of the day on every First Friday. Obviously, this would be a most appropriate occasion for the making of the Holy Hour. Points of Meditation and prayers assigned at the end of this book may be read aloud, in a clear, distinct voice, leaving pauses of silence for private reflection and prayer, and concluding with Benediction of the Blessed Sacrament.

A short instruction given previously on some subject connected with the Holy Hour would add much to the devotion of those present.

The introduction at intervals during the hour of music and hymns to the Sacred Heart in which all assembled took part, would also do much to inspire fervor, and would add an element of attractiveness and variety to the exercises of the Holy Hour.

All assisting at this devotion gain a Plenary Indulgence on the usual conditions.

N.B.—We cannot too strongly recommend the public making of the Holy Hour somewhat after the manner just described, in presence of the Blessed Sacrament exposed, on the First Friday of each month. This practice will be found to be fraught with unspeakable blessings and graces in all Parishes, Convents, and Schools where it is adopted.

The Practice in Private.

The Holy Hour may be made in private in any place and at any time. But to gain the Plenary Indulgence, it must, if done privately, be made between the hours of two o'clock on Thursday afternoon and sunrise on Friday morning.

No set form of prayer or meditation is essential; any of the methods suggested at the end of this book may be adopted. Though desirable, it is not necessary* that it should be made in the presence of the Blessed Sacrament. Hence the sick and infirm who are unable to leave their homes may make the Holy Hour and gain all its advantages at home.

Priests and the Holy Hour.

There is no manifest reason why priests and others bound to the recitation of the *Divine Office* should not become entitled, under the conditions laid down, to all the advantages of the Holy Hour by uniting their Office with the prayer of Christ in the Garden and offering it for the other intentions already specified. The making of the Holy Hour in this way involves no extra expenditure of time, and it will be found to be a powerful help towards the fervent recitation of the Divine Office, a means of fostering devotion to the Sacred Heart, and to the Passion, and in general a strong incentive to fervor and devotion.

Religious Communities and the Holy Hour.

Religious communities have got special facilities for making the Holy Hour, whether all together in public, or, as individuals, in private.

We have no hesitation in promising an abundant outpouring of Divine grace, together with a marked increase in the religious spirit, especially in the virtue of charity and in the fervent observance of religious discipline, in those communities that adopt the practice of the Holy Hour.

In many communities the beautiful custom of having Exposition of the Blessed Sacrament on the First Friday has been already established, with the most consoling results, and there is every prospect of its being still more widely spread and encouraged on all sides.

The Ordinary Faithful and the Holy Hour.

Persons living in the world will find in the Holy Hour a source of strength and consolation. It will do much to make their lives more spiritual and to draw them closer to God. They may at this time recommend to God all their spiritual and temporal concerns and invoke the blessing of the Sacred Heart upon their family and friends.

VII. METHODS OF MAKING THE HOLY HOUR

FIRST METHOD: BY MEDITATION

First Quarter-of-an-hour.

1st **Prelude.**—Listen to our Divine Lord saying: "My soul is sorrowful even unto death."

2nd **Prelude.**—Sweet Jesus help me to understand the depth of Thy sorrow and to be filled with deep compassion.

First Meditation.

Then Jesus came with them into a country place which is called Gethsemani, and He said to His disciples: Sit you here till I go yonder and pray. And taking with Him Peter and the two sons of Zebedee, He began to grow sorrowful and to be sad,—Matthew. xxvi. 36-37.

FIRST POINT.

Consideration.—Jesus calls us aside from the crowded thoroughfare of worldly aspirations and pursuits that, like Peter and the sons of Zebedee, we, too, may bear Him company in His most bitter agony. What a privilege! How happy ought I to be to keep my dear Lord company in His hour of sorest trial.

But see, His mortal anguish is upon Him. *"He begins to grow sorrowful and to be sad."* What are the causes of His sorrow? There are two causes: (1) The keen and vivid perception of the sufferings and cruel death He is about to undergo. The profound humiliations He should suffer at the various tribunals, the agonizing torture of the scourging, and of the cruel crowning with thorns, the dolorous journey to Mount Calvary, the horrible nailing of His Hands and Feet, the awful agony upon the Cross—all were clearly present to His Mind in their minutest details. (2) And more appalling still was the dreadful vision of the sins of men. The Savior, who shrank with such unutterable shrinking from the slightest breath of sin, beheld Himself plunged in, and deluged with, a very ocean of iniquity. All the nameless horrors and enormities perpetrated in the course of ages by the human race, the sins that called the universal deluge from the heavens, the shameful crimes of Sodom and Gomorrah, all the unnatural excesses of the Pagan world, the far more inexcusable excesses of the Christian era, rising up before Him, in a never-ending vista of iniquity, overwhelmed and crushed the weary fainting spirit of the Savior and forced the very blood to ooze in ruddy streams from every pore.

Application,—And my sins, too, are there among that black array, and I have had a part in inflicting all these cruel sufferings on my loving Savior. Shall I not now try to make amends by the loving assiduity with which I try to keep our Lord company in this Holy Hour and thus assuage the bitter sorrows of His soul.

Affections and Resolutions.—O, my Lord, I am sorry from the bottom of my heart for the share I have had in causing Thy bitter agony in the Garden. My God, I offer up to Thee the infinite merits of Christ, His Life of labor, the sufferings of His Passion and His cruel Death in atonement for my own sins and for those of all mankind. "Look upon the Face of thy Christ."

Spare, O Lord! spare Thy people, and be not angry with us forever *(three times).*

Recite the Act of Contrition.

SECOND POINT.

Then He saith to them: My soul is sorrowful even unto death.—Matthew. xxvi. 38.

Consideration.—The bitter anguish of His Soul finds vent in words of gentle lamentation and complaint to His disciples. Is there not something very touching in the fact of our Lord's thus, as it were, seeking consolation from His own creatures? It is so natural, so human, so like what we should do ourselves. To you and me, now, as we kneel here making the Holy Hour, He whispers, down in the depths of our souls, the self-same words: "My *soul is sorrowful even unto death,* and I want you to console Me."

Application.—We too have, each of us, our hours of sorrow and desolation, when bitterness and disappointment take possession of the heart, when the past is as a vision that has vanished in the night, and the future is a dreary waste of darkness and uncertainty. Let us then reflect how Jesus' soul was sorrowful even unto death and unite the sorrows of our soul with His.

Affections and Resolutions—O Lord, I wish to keep Thee company in Thy sorrow, I unite my little pains and griefs with Thine. Teach me to bear them patiently for Thy sake.

Spare, O Lord, spare Thy people, and be not angry with us forever *(three times)*.

Pater, Ave, and *Gloria (thrice)* for the conversion of sinners.

THIRD POINT.

Stay you here and watch with Me.—Matthew xxvi. 38.

Consideration.—It is thus our Lord appeals to us: *"Stay you here and watch with Me."* Long before, by the mouth of the Psalmist, He had said: *"I looked for one that would grieve together with Me, but there was none: and for one that would comfort Me, and I found none "* (Psalm lxviii. 21). Do you at least stay here "that you may be the witness of My agony, and in every tribulation you may learn like Me to have recourse to prayer, that by watching with Me, suffering with Me, praying with Me, you may bring some solace and relief to My afflicted Heart" (a Lapide).

Application.—Be not deaf to the appeal of Christ, but esteem it your highest privilege to bear Him company in His affliction.

Affections and Resolutions.—My God, grant me the grace of persevering, humble prayer, especially in times of sorrow and affliction.

Spare, O Lord, spare Thy people, and be not angry with us for ever *(thrice)*.

Pater, Ave, and *Gloria (thrice)* for those in their last agony.

Second Quarter-of-an-hour.

Second Meditation.

1st Prelude.—See Christ prostrate with His face to the earth.

2nd Prelude.—O Lord, enable me to realize the intensity of Thy anguish, and to imitate Thy conformity to the will of God.

FIRST POINT.

And going a little farther, He fell upon His Face, praying, and saying: My Father, if it be possible, let this chalice pass from Me.—Matthew xxvi. 39,

Consideration.—*He fell upon His face.*—(1) To show the depth of His affliction ; (2) to give us an example of humility and of profound respect towards God in prayer; (3) to let us see the enormity and weight of our iniquities which thus pressed Him down to the very earth; (4) that thus laden with the sins of men, and clothed with their iniquities, He might offer Himself a living Holocaust and victim of expiation for the human race.

Father, if it be possible, let this chalice pass away. It is the cry of Christ's human nature, shrinking back in terror from the chalice of suffering that awaited Him, yet perfectly resigned and submissive to His Eternal Father's Will.

Application.—Imagine you see Christ offering you this same chalice and inviting you to drink of it with Him, by bearing your cross patiently along with Him. Answer Him in the words of Psalm cxv.: *"I will take the chalice of salvation"*; and that you may have strength to do so, add: *"And I will call upon the name of the Lord."*

Affections and Resolutions.—"Lest I should be overcome by adversity, O Lord, let Thy power strengthen me, Thy charity inflame my zeal, Thy wisdom fill me, Thy constancy confirm me" (St. Bernard).

Spare, O Lord, spare Thy people, and be not angry with us forever *(thrice)*.

Pater, Ave, and *Gloria (thrice)* for sinners who are to die today.

SECOND POINT.

Yet not My will, but Thine be done.—Luke xxii. 42.

Consideration.—"The human will of Christ," says a Lapide, "was virtually twofold; the one natural, whereby He shrank from death, the other rational and free, whereby submitting Himself to the Divine Will, He welcomed death with the words: *Not My will but Thine be done."*

Application.—When you feel crushed down and well-nigh fainting beneath the load of trouble and anxiety, when you are overwhelmed with sorrow, when some sudden affliction overtakes you, say with your lips, if you cannot do so with your heart: *Not my will but Thine be done, O Lord!*

Affections and Resolutions.—O Lord, enable me to imitate Thy courage, firmness, and constancy in embracing in all things the most holy will of God.

Spare, O Lord, spare Thy people, and be not angry with us forever *(thrice}*.

Pater, Ave, and *Gloria (thrice)* for the conversion of pagan nations, especially Japan.

THIRD POINT.

He went again, and He prayed the third time, saying the self-same word.—Matthew xxvi. 44.

Consideration.—*He prayed the third time.*—(1) To show the vehemence of His sorrow; (2) to teach us to persevere in prayer. "If Christ was not heard by His Father on His first or second prayer," says a Lapide, "what wonder if your prayers do not at once receive an answer."

Saying the self-same Word.—We oftentimes complain of our inability to pray. But if we cannot make profound reflections or elicit varied aspirations and affections we can always "say *the selfsame word,*" repeating the same petition again and again, and dwelling on it with renewed intensity.

Application.—Never shall we have such difficulties to contend against in prayer as Christ had in the Garden. Yet, in spite of tedium, of the most terrible aridity, of physical exhaustion and depression, He persevered, and, single-handed and unaided by the presence or sympathy of His Apostles, He fought and overcame the powers of darkness.

Affections and Resolutions —O Lord, make me valiant and persevering in prayer.

Spare, O Lord, spare Thy people, and be not angry with us forever *{thrice)*.

Pater, Ave, and *Gloria (thrice)* for the grace of a happy death for ourselves.

Third Quarter-of-an-hour.

Third Meditation.

1st Prelude.—Christ in agony and the angel comforting Him.

2nd Prelude.—Ask grace to join with the angel in consoling our Lord.

FIRST POINT.

And being in an agony He prayed the longer.—Luke xxii. 43.

Consideration.—(1) We find it hard at times to remain even for some short time in prayer, and, yielding to the dryness and difficulty we feel, we abandon the attempt. How different is the conduct of our Lord! (2) A hard, dry, difficult prayer, made only with great effort, is oftentimes the best.

Application.—Persevere in making the Holy Hour, even though you find it hard.

Affections and Resolutions.—O Lord, in honor and in memory of Thy prayer and agony, help me to bear Thee company in Thy afflictions.

Spare, O Lord, spare Thy people, and be not angry with us forever *(thrice}*.

Pater, Ave, and *Gloria (thrice)* for the grace of a happy death for all our relatives and friends.

SECOND POINT.

And His sweat became as drops of blood trickling down upon the ground.—Luke xxii. 44.

Consideration.—To what a pitiable condition have my sins reduced the Savior. The intensity of His agony, the horror that filled and crushed His Sacred Heart at the awful vision of sin, the violent effort to overcome the shrinking of His Human Nature from the sufferings that awaited Him—all combined to force the very Blood out through the pores of His Body until It ran trickling down in great red drops and formed in pools, or drenched the moss-covered ground on which He lay.

Application.—Christ sweats blood for love of me, shall I refuse Him the tribute of my sweat in laboring in His behalf to make atonement for my sins?

Affections and Resolutions.—O Lord, my soul is as a vineyard planted by Thy Hand, but overgrown, alas, with weeds and briars, and sterile in good works; but with Thy Precious Blood Thou hast deigned to water it and make it fertile. O grant me grace to love Thee in return for such love.

Spare, O Lord, spare Thy people, and be not angry with us forever *(thrice)*.

Pater, Ave, and *Gloria (thrice)* for the souls in purgatory.

THIRD POINT

And there appeared to Him an angel from heaven strengthening Him.—Luke xxii. 43.

Consideration.—It is your privilege in making the Holy Hour to join with the angel in comforting and consoling our afflicted Savior. Among the motives for consolation pointed out to Christ by the angel, we may believe that he showed our Lord those souls who in future ages would strive to console His Sacred Heart by their assiduity and fervor in meditating on His Passion, bearing Him company in His prayer and agony in the Garden, and offering Him a loving tribute of sympathy and compassion with Him in His sorrow and abandonment.

Application.—Am I among the number of those, the vision of whose future fidelity and devotion to His Passion, especially in the exercises of the Holy Hour, acted as an influence to "strengthen" and console Him in His dereliction?

Affections and Resolutions.—O my Lord and Savior, agonizing in the Garden, allow me, poor wretched sinner though I be, to join humbly with the angel in offering to Thee during this Holy Hour whatever consolation it is in my power to give Thee.

Spare, O Lord, etc., and prayers as heretofore.

Fourth Quarter-of-an-hour.

Fourth Meditation.

1st Prelude.—Hear Christ saying to you: " Could you not watch one hour with Me?" Matthew XXVI. 40.

2nd Prelude.—Lord, grant me grace to understand, love, and practice the devotion of the Holy Hour.

FIRST POINT.

And He cometh to His disciples, and findeth them asleep, and He saith to Peter: What! could you not watch one hour with Me?—Matthew xxvi. 40.

Consideration.—How it pained the Heart of our Divine Lord to find such want of sympathy with Him in His hour of greatest sorrow, especially as He had asked them but a short time before to "Stay you here and watch with Me." To us, too, when oftentimes He comes and finds us "sleeping" in the sleep of tepidity and slothfulness, he addresses the self-same words of sadness and disappointment: "Could you not watch one hour with Me?"

Application.—Let us, at least, strive not to merit this reproach. How much we shall do to assuage the bitterness of disappointment that filled the gentle Heart of Christ on this occasion, if we are devoted to the practice of the Holy Hour.

Affections and Resolutions.—O my loving Savior, grant me grace to "*watch*" with Thee, my heart inflamed with love, and full of tender sympathy and compassion for Thee in Thy bitter agony.

Spare, O Lord, spare Thy people, and be not angry with us forever *(thrice).*

Pater, Ave, and *Gloria (thrice)* for the spread of the beautiful practice of the Holy Hour.

SECOND POINT.

Watch ye and pray that ye enter not into temptation. The spirit indeed is willing but the flesh is weak.—Matthew xxvi. 41.

Consideration.—Watchfulness and prayer. These are our two great duties that we may not "enter into temptation"—that is, as St. Jerome explains, that temptation may not overcome us and involve us in the toils of sin. The disciples failed in this watchfulness, and, therefore, when the time of trial came, "they all fled."

Application.—Though the spirit be willing, yet we fall far short of our good desires and resolutions, owing to the weakness of the flesh—*i.e.,* of our poor frail nature, whose inherent weakness must be overcome and fortified by prayer.

Affections and Resolutions.—Grant me the grace, O Lord, to watch with Thee in prayer, that in time of trial and temptation I may not abandon Thee.

Spare, O Lord, spare Thy people, and be not angry with us forever *(thrice)*.

Pater, Ave, and *Gloria (thrice)* for the intentions of all those making this Holy Hour.

THIRD POINT.

And when He returned He found them again asleep.— Mark xiv. 40.

Consideration.—Again asleep ! in spite of all His earnest appeals to them to watch and keep Him company in His intense sorrow. Who can picture the bitter grief that pierced the Heart of Christ at this utter neglect and indifference of His Apostles? The only little sign of sympathy and compassion He had demanded of them in His bitter agony was refused. Oh! how lonely and desolate and heart-broken did our poor Lord feel at this fresh instance of indifference on the part of the only friends He had remaining!

Application.—Shall we not, in view of this intensified neglect of the Apostles, redouble our efforts to console Him? If ever we are treated in like manner by our friends let us think of what our Lord suffered and unite our sorrow with His.

Affections and Resolutions.—Slightly changing the words of St. Peter say very humbly and with great affection: "O, my dear Lord, though all should leave Thee I will never abandon Thee"; and pray that it may be so.

Spare, O Lord, spare Thy people, and be not angry with us forever *(thrice)*.

Pater, Ave, and *Gloria (thrice)* for all the intentions of the Church and of the Pope.

N.B.—For those who are adepts at meditation one or two of the meditations given above will suffice to occupy the hour, leaving the others for the next occasion. If the meditations are read aloud one point may be read every five minutes, leaving a pause after each point for reflection and prayer in silence, and concluding with the prayers assigned which are recited aloud. Thus, each quarter-of-an-hour will be occupied by a separate meditation divided into three points. Excellent meditations for the Holy Hour will also be found among those already given in the earlier portion of this work.

SECOND METHOD OF MAKING THE HOLY HOUR

OFFICE OF THE PASSION.

Office of the Passion.

(Translated from the Latin.)

Matins

First Quarter-of-an-hour.

By the sign of the Cross save us from our enemies. O God!

V. Open my lips, O Lord!

R. And my tongue shall announce Thy praise.

V. Incline unto my aid, O God!

R. O Lord, make haste to help me.

V. Glory be to the Father, and to the Son, and to the Holy Ghost.

R. As it was in the beginning, is now, and ever shall be, world without end. Amen.

Alleluia.

Hymn.

At Matin song the Savior of the world

Is seized, while night still drapes the silent earth;

His faithless friends abandon Him and fly;

Neglected, sold, betrayed, He stands alone,

Unfriended in the presence of His foes.

Antiphon.—O Venerable Cross that didst bring salvation to us wretched sinners, how shall I sufficiently extol Thee, seeing that Thou hast procured for us eternal life!

V. We adore Thee, O Christ and bless Thee.

R. Because by Thy Holy Cross Thou hast redeemed the world.

Let us Pray.

O Lord Jesus Christ! Son of the living God, place Thy Cross, Passion, and Death between Thy judgment and my soul now and at the hour of my death; vouchsafe, O Lord! to grant to me grace and mercy, to the living and the dead rest and pardon, to Thy Church peace and concord, and to all of us sinners, life and glory everlasting. Who livest and reignest world without end. *R. Amen.*

Prime.

By the sign of the Cross save us from our enemies, O God!

Incline unto my aid, etc.

Glory be to the Father, etc. *Alleluia.*

Hymn.

At hour of Prime they bring the Lord of all Before the

Roman Governor, and there False witnesses against

His life conspire, A brutal soldier strikes Him on the

Face, On which the very angels fear to gaze.

Antiphon.—O Cross, triumphant, glorious standard, enable us to win our triumphs in the courts above.

V. We adore Thee, O Christ, etc., *with prayer as before* (see above).

Terse.

By the sign of the Cross save us from our enemies, O God!

Incline unto my aid, etc.

Glory be to the Father, etc. *Alleluia.*

Hymn.

At hour of Terse the brutal cry resounds From Jewish
lips of "Crucify Him," while They clothe Him in a
purple robe of shame, And place a thorny crown upon
His Head, And load Him, fainting, with the heavy Cross.

Antiphon.—The cruel sentence of death is passed upon that Christ Who broke for us, upon the Cross, the bonds of sin.

We adore Thee, O Christ! etc., *with prayer as before* (p. 150).

Sext.

By the sign of the Cross save us from our enemies, O God!
Incline unto my aid, etc.
Glory be to the Father, etc. *Alleluia.*

Hymn.

At hour of Sext they nail Him to the Cross And place
Him hanging in the midst of thieves, They give Him
gall and vinegar to drink, And mock Him as Ho hangs
in bitter woe For three long cruel hours on the Cross.

Antiphon.—By the fruit of the tree we were made slaves, and by Thy Holy Cross we are set free. The fruit of the tree was our destruction. The Son of God hath redeemed us.

V. We adore Thee, O Christ, etc., *with prayer as before* (p. 150).

None.

By the sign of the Cross save us from our enemies, O God!
Incline unto my aid, O God .. etc.
Glory be to the Father, etc. *Alleluia.*

Hymn.

At hour of None our Loving Savior dies. And with a
full-voiced cry gives up His Soul Into His Father's
Hands; with cruel lance His side is pierced, and forth
in ruddy drops, Come Blood and Water, mingled,
from His Heart.

Antiphon.—O mighty work of our redemption ! Death itself was overthrown when He Who was true Life itself laid down His life upon the Cross.

We adore Thee, O Christ. etc., *with prayer as before* (p. 150).

Vespers.

By the sign of the Cross save us from our enemies, O God!

Incline unto my aid, O God! etc.

Glory be to the Father, etc. *Alleluia.*

Hymn.

At Vesper song they take His Body down, And
gently lay It in the Mother's arms, The Queen of
Sorrows gazes on Her Son;
As co-redemptrix of the human race
Her heart is pierced with seven swords of grief.

Antiphon.—O blessed Cross I that alone wast worthy to bear the world's Redeemer; blessed wood and blessed nails that bore so sweet a burden; thou alone, O noble Cross, art more exalted than the cedar-tree, thou on whom the Savior of the world hung, whereon Christ won His victory, and by His death conquered death for ever.

We adore Thee, O Christ! etc., *with prayer as before* (p. 150).

Compline.

By the sign of the Cross save us from our enemies, O God!

Incline unto my aid, O God! etc.

Glory be to the Father, etc. *Alleluia.*

Hymn.

When Compline sounds they carry to the tomb The
Sacred Body carefully embalmed By loving hands,
and place a mighty stone, Roll'd close against the
door, and go their way In silent grief, to keep the parasceve.

Antiphon.—O Savior of the world ! save us, who by Thy Cross and Passion hast redeemed us. Come unto our aid, O God! we beseech Thee.

We adore Thee, O Christ! etc., *with prayer as before* (p. 150).

Second Quarter-of-an-hour.

Act of Reparation and Act of Consecration to the Sacred Heart, Litany of the Sacred Heart. "Spare, O Lord! spare Thy people," etc. *(thrice).* Prayer in silence.

Third Quarter-of-an-hour.

Sorrowful mysteries of the Rosary for Sinners in their last agony. "Spare, O Lord! spare Thy people," etc. *(thrice).* Prayer in silence.

Fourth Quarter-of-an-hour.

Benediction of the Blessed Sacrament or Stations of the Cross (if made in common);
Or (if made in private):
Pater, Ave, and *Gloria Patri* five times in honor of the Five Wounds, for the intentions of the Sacred Heart. *Pater, Ave, Credo* thrice in honor of the Three Hours' Agony on the Cross for the conversion of sinners. "Spare, O Lord! spare Thy people" etc. *(thrice).* Prayer in silence.

Other Prayers Suitable for the Holy Hour

The following prayers will be found in most prayer-books, and are very suitable for the Holy Hour: The Litany of the Passion, Litany of the Sacred Heart, Litany of Jesus, Acts of Reparation and Consecration to the Sacred Heart, Acts of Reparation to the Blessed Sacrament, Acts of Contrition, *Anima Christi, En Ego, De Profundis, Miserere, Stabat Mater, Confiteor,* Consecration of Families to the Sacred Heart, Stations of the Cross, etc. Many beautiful prayers most suitable for the Holy Hour will also be found in the excellent little prayer-book, entitled *Child of Mary before Jesus abandoned! (Messenger* Office, Dublin), price 6d. to 2s. 6d., according to binding.

Hymns.

If there be singing during the Holy Hour, hymns such as the following may be sung: *Pange Lingua, Stabat Mater,* "To Jesus' Heart all Burning!" "Jesus, the very thought of Thee," (O *Salutaris, Tantum Ergo,* various hymns to the Sacred Heart, etc.

(See *Book of Hymns to the Sacred Heart,* price 2d.; also hymns in leaflet form, to be had at the *Messenger* Office, London or Dublin.)

An Hour with Thee.

"My heart is tired, so tired to-night, How endless seems the strife!

Day after day the restlessness

Of all this weary life!

I come to lay my burden down, That so oppresseth me,

And, shutting all the world without, To spend an hour with Thee, dear Lord, To spend

an hour with Thee."

THE END